PENGUIN BOOKS

THE LAW OF DELAY

Born in 1909, Cyril Northcote Parkinson comes originally from Barnard Castle, County Durham, and was educated at St Peter's School, York, and at the Universities of Cambridge and London. Since then he has had a varied career as painter, teacher, soldier, journalist, and author. A Fellow at one time of Emmanuel College, Cambridge, he was Raffles Professor of History at the University of Malaya from 1950 to 1958. He has taught since then at Harvard, Illinois, and the University of California at Berkeley. He claims to have learnt his first lessons in administration when serving on the General Staff during World War II. All three services, however, combined to provide him with the experience upon which his first famous Law was based. He is married, with five children all told, and lives in Guernsey when not travelling, as he often does, in the U.S.A. and on the Continent.

Until *Parkinson's Law* was published in 1957 his authorship was confined to historical works such as *Trade in the Eastern Seas* (1937), *The Rise of the Port of Liverpool* (1952) and *War in the Eastern Seas* (1955). Since then his satirical works, *The Law and the Profits* (1960) and *In-Laws and Outlaws* (1962), have alternated with such serious books as *The Evolution of Political Thought* (1958) and *East and West* (1963). His most recent books are *The Life and Times of Horatio Hornblower* (1970), *Devil to Pay* (1973), *Big Business* (1974), *The Fireship* (1974), *Gunpowder, Treason and Plot* (1976) and *The Rise of Big Business* (1977).

C. Northcote Parkinson

THE LAW OF DELAY

Interviews and Outerviews

ILLUSTRATIONS
BY OSBERT LANCASTER

Penguin Books

Penguin Books Ltd, Harmondsworth, Middlesex, England
Penguin Books, 625 Madison Avenue, New York, New York 10022, U.S.A.
Penguin Books Australia Ltd, Ringwood, Victoria, Australia
Penguin Books Canada Ltd, 2801 John Street, Markham, Ontario, Canada L3R 1B4
Penguin Books (N.Z.) Ltd, 182–190 Wairau Road, Auckland 10, New Zealand

—

First published by John Murray 1970
Published in Penguin Books 1978

—

—

Made and printed in Great Britain by
Cox & Wyman Ltd, London, Reading and Fakenham
Set in Monotype Bembo

for Charles

Contents

Preface

The essays here reprinted have appeared over the years in different periodicals, some inspired by a particular occasion, others representing my response to an editorial request. The vague theme, just discoverable, is that rulers and ruled have drifted dangerously apart. We see on every side the public demonstration, the procession of protest, the expression of hate. We also see the mere size and complexity of the institutions which overshadow our modern world: political and industrial bureaucracies are all seemingly beyond our power to influence or even penetrate. Some conclude from this that riot is the only remedy. If this conclusion is wrong it is for our rulers to prove it by forming new organizations on a more human scale. In the comparison I have sought to make in one of these essays between one country and another, it is the smaller countries which gain the higher marks. There is a proportionate size which goes with maximum efficiency and all our institutions tend to exceed it.

If there is a proper size for a unit of administration, whether industrial or public, there is also a proper size for a book of essays; I owe much in this respect to the sage counsel of my publisher. I owe as much again to the genius of Mr Osbert Lancaster, whose satirical eye takes in the essence of every situation, perceiving the folly of the rebel but noting, as pitilessly, the awful complacency of those who rule. My illustrator can suggest more with a few flicks of the pencil than a mere author can hope to convey in as many volumes. While I can claim credit for my discovery of the Law of Delay, I have to admit it is by his immortal drawing that the Law will be remembered.

I have also to express my gratitude to the several Editors and organizations who have given me permission to reprint the essays which first appeared in their respective magazines, often in a rather different form: *Daily Telegraph Magazine*, chapters 1 and 2; *Homes and Gardens*, 3; *Economist*, 4; *Lords*, 5; *Illustrated London News*, 6, 9, 10; *Think*, 12; *The Times Business Section*, 14. The three figures in Chapter 4 were made by the *Economist* from my original drawings, and are here re-produced by kind permission of the Editor. I am particularly grateful to Rank Xerox Ltd for permission to include Chapter 13. It is based on an article, commissioned by them, which appeared in a special supplement of *The Times*.

I must add my personal thanks to those who have helped prepare the book for press, and especially to Miss Marjorie Caton-Jones who did much of the research, and Mrs Kate Green, my secretary, who deciphered my handwriting and made the typescript. To Charles this book is dedicated because upon him I can rely for healthy argument. After discussion of any point within the family circle I can always feel that I have heard the opposite point of view. Having heard it, I am still more confident, of course, that I was right in the first place.

To Ann I have more than thanks to express and no words in which to record my indebtedness. Her partnership is to be assumed in all I have done and upon it I rely for all I still hope to achieve.

C. NORTHCOTE PARKINSON

Guernsey, February 1970

Chapter 1

TEN YEARS AFTER

Parkinson's Law was first published in Britain in 1958, the central theme of its key chapter suggesting that a Civil Service expands by an inexorable rule of growth, irrespective of the work (if any) which has to be done. The examples quoted were taken from the Admiralty and Colonial Office, these two Ministries revealing in each case an annual 5–6% staff increase, during a period of manifest decline in naval strength and col-

onial activity. Ten years have passed and it is fair to ask what the position is now. Do the statistics of the past decade go to substantiate or undermine the theory first propounded? This question is not easy to answer for official statistics are inconsistent, complex and obscure. There have been frequent reorganizations in which responsibilities and manpower have been shuffled back and forth between Colonial, Dominion and Foreign Offices. There has been the merger of the Armed Forces and of the Consular with the Diplomatic Corps. To discover what has happened is no easy task. Nor has the situation been unaffected by the author himself. If Karl Marx's predictions were falsified, in part, because his opponents had read his book, it may be true that *Parkinson's Law* has influenced the Select Committee on Estimates. Despite all confusion, however, and despite the impact of the book (as contrasted with the Law) there are grounds for regarding the author as a true prophet.

Take the Admiralty, to begin with, as our first and classic example of administrative proliferation:

	1914	1928	Increase or Decrease
Total number of vessels in commission	542	317	−41·51%
Officers and men in RN	125,000	90,700	−27·44%
Dockyard workers	57,000	62,439	+9·54%
Dockyard officials and clerical staff	3,249	4,558	+40·28%
Admiralty officials and clerical staff	4,366	7,729	+77·03%

The subsequent story, up to the merger and for a later year (1967), would read as follows:

	1938	1948	1958	1964	1967
Total number of vessels	308	413	238	182	114
Officers and men	89,500	134,400	94,900	84,900	83,900

	1938	1948	1958	1964	1967
Dockyard workers	39,022	48,252	40,164	41,563	37,798
Dockyard officials and clerical staff	4,423	6,120	6,219	7,395	8,013
Admiralty officials and clerical staff	11,270	31,636	32,237	32,035	33,574

The conclusion from this research would be that the 5·5% annual growth of the admiralty staff (calculated arithmetically on the base year) between 1914 and 1928 was replaced by a 9·3% growth between 1938 and 1958, and whereas 1914 represented the culmination of an arms race, when 4,366 officials could administer what was then the largest navy in the world, 1967 represents the point at which we have become practically powerless, by which period over 33,000 civil servants are barely sufficient to administer the navy we no longer possess. Negligible as we may be in world politics, we can still deploy administrative forces in Bath, Whitehall, Queen Anne's Mansions, Rex House, Kidbrooke, Cricklewood, Harrow and the Charing Cross Road. For any weakness observable at Singapore or Malta we may console ourselves with the thought that our base at Northwood Hills (Pinner) is virtually impregnable. It would be wrong, incidentally, to suppose that the Naval Division of the Ministry of Defence brought to that headquarters a habit of administrative expansion which was alien to the other Services. The War Office, for one, need never shirk comparison with the Admiralty. In 1935 a civilian staff of 9,442 sufficed to administer an Army reduced to 203,361 officers and men; the low-water mark of unpreparedness for a conflict which was by then obviously inevitable. By 1966 a civilian staff of 48,032 was giving encouragement to some 187,100 men in uniform, a 7·9% reduction in fighting strength being accompanied by a

408% increase in paperwork. It might be rash, however, to
surmise that an annual 13·16% increase in civilian staff is normal to the War Office. We have rather to realize that merger
with Navy and Air Force tripled the volume of correspondence
as from the first day and that further progression is more likely
to be on a geometric than on a merely arithmetic scale. If we
thus plot on a graph the curve of expansion for the Admiralty
Division of the Ministry of Defence we find that its civilian
staff should number about 72,000 by 1984,* in which year there
should of course be no Navy of any kind. By the same year the
military division of the same Ministry should number about
124,000.

Our second example of administrative growth was taken
from the Colonial Office, the figures quoted being as follows:

1935	1939	1943	1947	1954
173	450	817	1139	1661

For the same years the combined total of the Colonial,
Dominion, India and Burma Offices was as follows:

1023	1075	1709	2362	2650

Various reorganizations prevent us giving any more recent
totals than for 1957 (2,743) and for 1960 (2,827). We need to
remember, however, that the period covered by these statistics,
from 1935 to the present day, is notable for the collapse of our
empire; a collapse for which there is hardly a parallel in history.
From 1947, more especially, we can list as follows the territories
which gained their independence: India, Pakistan, Ceylon,
Ghana, Malaysia, Cyprus, Nigeria, Sierra Leone, Tanzania,
Jamaica, Trinidad and Tobago, Uganda, Kenya, Malawi,

* Why 1984? Why not?

Malta, Zambia, Gambia, Singapore, Guyana, Botswana, Lesotho and Barbados.

Each newly independent territory has meant the loss of a governorship and the gain of an embassy. Whereas our ambassadors numbered only 16 in 1940 they now number over 80 with High Commissioners as well and representatives accredited to NATO, SEATO, and UNO. A 412·5% increase in the number of embassies might seem to justify a 378·23% increase in the staff of the Foreign Service. Whether that was the actual increase must remain doubtful however, because there are, in this instance, four different sets of figures to choose from; one from the Treasury, one from the Foreign Office News Department, another from Civil Estimates and the last from the Diplomatic Service Administration Office. Of these guesses the first has been preferred but it differs from the last by about 7,000. Whether those employed in Whitehall have ever been actually counted must remain a question and it is just as difficult to obtain a precise estimate of those recruited locally overseas. In so far, however, as the figures can be trusted at all, the Foreign Office/Diplomatic Service would seem to have been heavily reinforced since 1940, the following figures giving at least a vague indication of the recent trend:

1935	1940	1945	1950	1955	1960	1965	1967
1,412	2,270	6,806	6,195	5,670	5,992	10,211	10,856

The sudden increase recorded for 1965 was not due to a diplomatic crisis but to an amalgamation with the Commonwealth Relations Office, which had itself risen in strength from 651 (in 1935) to 1,729 (in 1964). Such reorganizations apart, the tale of expansion is highly impressive. If mere numbers could achieve anything, our current representation overseas should signify an almost overwhelming influence on world affairs.

From the varying and dubious figures we have quoted it will appear that Parkinson's Law has not been disproved over the past decade; least of all, perhaps, in the Ministries to which the author first drew attention. The trend of inevitable increase is certainly proved from British experience. What is more doubtful is the preliminary guess that annual peacetime staff accumulation may average 5·75%. This prediction was qualified, remember, by the reminder that 'new developments occur almost daily' and that all estimates be regarded as tentative. Granted that this is so, and that further research remains to be done, the fact remains that the author's first guess was not too wide of the mark. Whereas the Ministries vary in their rate of staff accumulation, the average annual increase in five of them would work out as shown in the table below for the period 1935–66.

Of this increase, however, a part is attributable to an actual increase of work. The population of Britain rose from 45,598,000 in 1935 to 53,266,000 in 1966, justifying a 16·8% increase in the cost of administration, an annual increase of 0·5% per year. Taxation was made steadily more onerous and complex and bureaucratic interference with trade became

Ministry	1935	1966	% annual increase
Home Office and Prison Commission	4,350	16,066	8·68
Inland Revenue	22,851	59,502	5·17
War Office	9,442	48,032	13·18
Board of Trade	4,328	9,598	3·92
Air Ministry	5,481	24,848	11·39
Average annual increase			8·49

habitual. We are frequently at war on a minor scale and the

financial problem of reconciling this with vote-catching welfare measures made perpetual difficulties for the Civil Service. With more people in prison for contravening more obscure laws and regulations there was bound to be more work for the Home Office. In this way perhaps half of the annual increase might be explained, leaving 4·34% to be accounted for by the operation of Parkinson's Law. This falls short of the original estimate but we have to remember that Ministries have not merely grown but multiplied. The modest growth of the Board of Trade is thus due to the establishment of the parallel Ministries of Transport and Technology. If allowance is made for these developments, the inevitable growth – apart from any increase in work-load – may turn out to be very near the 5·75% of the original estimate. It will be manifest, however, that exact figures and percentages are almost unattainable.

What, however, of the Civil Service as a whole? Here again there are statistical difficulties due to reorganization and shifting areas of responsibility. There is a confused boundary between central and local government and a misty borderland between public service and nationalized industry. To make matters even more obscure there is no immutable distinction between industrial and non-industrial staff, a mere reclassification of grades in the Post Office being enough to alter the total by thousands. Within these shifting frontiers, however, the statistics – for what they are worth – read somewhat as follows:

1935	1940	1945	1950	1955	1960	1965
303,610	454,745	704,646	684,799	635,663	637,374	803,327

As on January 1, 1967, the total was 845,900, a not unimpressive share of the whole working population. This represents a 179% increase over the 32-year period or an annual average increase of 5·6%. That the percentage is not higher than that is due, in the first place, to the more modest demands of certain Ministries. That of Labour and National Service, for example, has actually declined since 1935 and nearly halved since 1943, much of its work being taken over by the Ministry of National Insurance. The Ministry of Transport has also halved since 1959. Such restraint, however, as there has been in other directions has been the result, clearly, of Parkinson's Law becoming known. The total of civil servants was actually reduced in 1955 – the year in which the essay first appeared – and was reduced again after the discovery was published in book form. Expansion began once more in 1960–65, after the initial impact of the book had been spent, and has continued ever since.

In the original essay (of 1955) much emphasis was placed on the purely scientific nature of the discovery there revealed, the author going so far as to observe that, 'It is not the business of the botanist to eradicate the weeds. Enough for him if he can tell us just how fast they grow.' It is surely appropriate that the present inquiry should be pursued in the same objective spirit. No attempt will be made, therefore, to decide whether 845,900 civil servants are too many or too few. We are justified, however, in plotting a curve to show what the result of the present rate of growth might be. By what date, we can fairly ask, should half the working population be absorbed in public administration? By what date, further, should the *whole* population have been so absorbed? For this purpose we need to include those employed in local as well as national affairs; a total of 1,077,050 public servants at the present time. Estimates reveal that these two dates are 2145 and 2195 respectively. It is no part of our present object to comment upon the new type of economy which will support such a way of life. That people should live by reading each other's memoranda is regarded, in official circles, as perfectly natural and feasible. There can be no doubt that the main features of the new economy have been foreseen and that planners are already studying their manifold implications. It is not for the private citizen, however, to venture into these realms of speculation. There are large and expanding departments devoted to blueprinting the coming Utopia and the whole subject is better left, therefore, to the experts.

Central to our system of administration and foremost in the march of progress is, of course, the Treasury. It is the Treasury that watches over the whole structure, ensuring that nothing is spent which could be saved and that nobody is employed whose services are not essential. Some comment upon the Treasury is to that extent inevitable and is the more needed in that one's mental picture of that institution is probably false. We think of the Treasury as comprising a small group of the dedicated and erudite, all from Winchester and New College and a few with some experience of the 60th Rifles. These are men, we imagine, of classical education whose sub-paragraphs are distinguished by letters from the Greek alphabet. They lunch at the Reform and do *The Times* crossword puzzle in a matter of seconds. They spend their evenings listening to classical music, their weekends at home in Hampstead Garden Suburb. They are, we tend to believe, at once powerful and obscure. Knowing that there are supposed to be about 200 of them, we may feel, as taxpayers, that never in the history of human extortion has so much been owed by so many to so few. Our preconceptions are largely based, however, upon errors of fact, and one such error concerns the numbers of the Treasury staff. This central Ministry may be small as compared with others but it is inferior to few in its speed of growth. The following figures may suffice to prove this point:

1935	1956	1966	Increase
309	1,249	1,639	430·42% or 13·88% p.a.

Among the old-established Ministries whose functions have not vastly altered only one, the War Office (with a 13·18%

increase per annum), can claim any comparable progress. From this point of view the expansion of, say, the Ministry of Technology has no statistical significance, being no more than the process which brought it into being. If we ignore such recent developments, as we surely ought, we must conclude that the Treasury leads the way. When we realize moreover that there has been a parallel growth of other offices concerned with finance, from the Ministry of Economic Affairs to the nationalized Bank of England, we might feel justified in making a total for them all. Such a calculation would place the Treasury far ahead of the field and in a class by itself.

While the Treasury has failed to hold down the numbers of the Civil Service, and has by its example encouraged proliferation, it has admittedly done something to limit the rising cost. The fact that the top civil servants have demanded, and obtained, something like the salaries paid to their industrial opposite numbers must not conceal from us the fact that their underlings are rather underpaid than otherwise. It is true that the total salary payments rose from £298 million in 1951 to £773 million in 1965. It is arguable, however, that the increase for the individual has barely kept pace with the dwindling value of the currency. Is the average pay per head in 1951 (£440) fairly represented, in purchasing power, by the average pay of 1965? This came to £1,057 and it offered, as an average, something very far short of wealth. Any industrial consultant might consider that double the salary would obtain more useful work from a quarter the number. That, however, is not to the present purpose, which is merely to record that the Treasury, failing dismally to restrain the rise in numbers, *can* claim a modest success in limiting the expense.

What, then, are we to think of the original prophecy? Civil servants *do* multiply by a law which governs their department's expansion. Work *does* expand so as to fill the time available.

Nor does the fact that people are busy prove that there is any-thing useful for them to do. We have no statistical proof, how-ever, for the theory that 5–6% per annum is the normal rate of staff-accumulation. It is not wildly off the mark but the vari-ations from this norm are at once frequent and unpredictable. It was the fashion among the early economists to explain what would happen in certain circumstances, a shortage causing a rise in price, a slack period causing a fall in wages. All these rules applied only to a free market, unaffected by governmental action or by combinations in restraint of trade; free, moreover, from civil disturbance or war. In the 20th Century the right circumstances never exist. There is a sense in which Parkinson's Law (or, to be exact, his first law) has suffered the same fate. The author postulated (very tentatively) a certain rate of ad-ministrative expansion in time of peace. He assumed the absence of any financial crisis or internal revolution. It is a question, however, whether these conditions have prevailed over the ten years we are considering or are likely to prevail over the ten years that lie ahead. This is not an age to which any very precise rules can be made to apply, least of all when the rules themselves have become generally known. His failure was in neglecting to make any allowance for the impact the theory was actually to have. Granted, however, that the Whitehall scene is confused by this factor among others, the basic fact remains that London (like Vienna) is now the disproportionately large capital of an empire that has ceased to exist. The headquarters of govern-ment was never designed as the administrative hub of the British Isles but as the centre of a spider's web which used to cover half the world. With that larger function gone, the Whitehall of today is not merely cumbersome but ludicrous. Reform may be impossible but we have still (so far) the right at least to laugh.

Chapter 2

THE PARKINSON PRIZE

The central problem of our time – from which our other difficulties mostly stem – is one produced by the stagnation of political theory during an age of technological advance. The most sophisticated machinery is thus placed in the hands of politicians whose ideas date from the era of the horse-drawn vehicle. They will happily argue the respective merits of democracy and dictatorship without making the slightest effort to ascertain the facts upon which their case (or any other case) might rest. In other words, the application of scientific method to political problems has hardly yet begun. When the approach is attempted, moreover, the first question propounded is one to which there can be no answer. 'What,' people ask, 'is the best form of rule?' But for whom, and where, and when? There is no likelihood, after all, that the same solution could apply to a score of different problems, nor indeed that the right answer now would be still correct in ten years' time. It would be more hopeful to ask, in the first place, what country is best administered today; and even this question is more difficult to answer than we might at first suppose. A full investigation would involve the deployment of great resources in money, skill and time. Even a tentative solution, however, based upon a more superficial inquiry, might be of some value as affording a tiny foothold of fact in a quagmire of misinformation, prejudice, guesswork and gas. For the attempt which follows the most that can be said is that the author has tried to be impartial, discarding every preconception and dealing only in facts which can be proved.

Were we to award a prize to the country which is best

governed, we would find, at the outset, that our field of inquiry is limited in two respects. We must omit from our tables of comparison some (not all) of the socialist countries beyond what are called the iron and bamboo curtains, not because we doubt their efficiency but because their relevant statistics are either unobtainable or are presented in a form which makes comparison difficult or impossible. We have to exclude, in the second place, some countries which are too small in population and area. Freely admitting that they may be admirably governed, we must, with apologies, ignore their existence. For were we to conclude, after careful study, that the world's most competent administrators are to be found in Monaco, Andorra, Seychelles and Sark, our findings would be of no great value to the folk who live in Australia, Britain, France or the USA. These last would object, and reasonably, that the problems which confront a small community are different in kind from those which surround the administration of a nation or continent. A comparative study must be of units which are at least roughly comparable in size.

With the list of countries thus curtailed we can apply to the remainder the first and obvious test of survival. If there is so high a death rate that waste and misery must result, so high a birth rate that the population tends to exceed what the country can support, so low an expectation of life that civilization must suffer, the country concerned cannot be listed among the more competent. It should be made clear, however, that this exclusion at the outset is no reflection (of necessity) on the country's present rulers. Starting, perhaps, from an infinitely weak position, they may have done wonders and may end for all we know in the forefront of progress. The fact remains, however, that their current level of efficiency is low. Countries with too high a death rate include Ghana (24·0 per 1,000), Kenya (20·0), Pakistan (15·4) and S.-W. Africa (15·2). Countries eliminated for excessive population increase – excluding those whose gain is by immigration – include Colombia, Ecuador, Fiji, Hong-Kong, Iraq, Jordan, Libya, Malaysia, Malta, the Philippines and Venezuela. Countries with an absurdly high birth rate – balanced admittedly by a high death rate – include Ceylon, Chile, El Salvador, Mexico, Nicaragua and Panama. Countries where people have an expectation of less than 55 years include – besides some of those already listed – Bolivia, Brazil, Burma, Haiti, India and Peru. Thirty-five countries remain but from some of these people seem to migrate in exceptional numbers. These figures may reflect a lack of space, as in Japan and Germany, but in other instances they would seem to reveal boredom or discontent, as in the Argentine, Australia, New Zealand and Spain. By way of a final test in the opening round, we must conclude that the annual suicide rates in Austria, Denmark, Czecho-Slovakia, and Hungary (all over 20 per 100,000 p.a.) are excessive and significant. We are thus left with the following countries:

Belgium	Netherlands
Canada	Norway
Finland	Portugal
France	South Africa
Germany	Sweden
Greece	Switzerland
Ireland	United Kingdom
Israel	United States
Luxembourg	Yugoslavia

All these relatively advanced countries have a good measure of prosperity and offer a fair expectation of life. In all, however, there are traffic risks which a competent administration would minimize. In this respect USA may be regarded as an exceptional case, with its high proportion of vehicles to population. With one vehicle to every 2·2 persons (1964), the American traffic problem is different in kind from that of Britain, say, with 5·2 persons per vehicle or that of Israel with 21. The American figure of 20·8 casualties per 1,000 vehicles is not, therefore, strictly comparable with the statistics of other countries. Where, however, the traffic density is not excessive and where the annual rate of fatal or serious casualties exceeds 15 per 1,000 vehicles or 30 per 10,000 of population, we may fairly conclude that more should have been done to make the roads safer. Application of this test must remove from the list Luxembourg (with 35·3 dead or injured per 10,000), Yugoslavia (with 32·2 per 1,000 vehicles), Switzerland (with 27·3 per 10,000 population), and Portugal (with 17·2 per 1,000 vehicles). Under this heading we might observe that Sweden is most safety-conscious of the countries for which statistics are available and appears to remain so even after the Swedes' unnatural and undemocratic decision to drive on the right of the road. Comparison of the statistics of safety in air travel might be as significant, but it is difficult, in practice, to decide what the figures mean. If a Norwegian jet liner (made in USA) crashes on a Belgian airfield, the accident could be due to the pilot's error or again to a mistake made in the control tower. Do we debit the casualties to Norway, Belgium or USA? Was the mishap due to the failure of an engine or a hole in the runway? Is it fair, for that matter, to compare the safety record of airlines operating over Europe with those submitted by airlines which fly over jungle or desert? At least initially, we do well to ignore statistics which defy analysis.

So far we have been dealing mainly with the elementary facts of survival and safety. In theory these should include considerations of defence but countries' needs in this respect are almost impossible to assess. The next logical basis, therefore, for comparison is in the general relationship between effort and results. Granted a fair level of competence and welfare, it is manifest that some countries pay too heavily for their administration. For the purposes of identifying these countries we have calculated the tax level in each, with the cost added of social security contributions, as a percentage of the gross national product. Our tentative conclusion is that a government which takes over 40% of the G.N.P. is asking too much for what it has to give. It is arguable, moreover, that the most costly administrations are not of necessity those which offer the most in terms of welfare. No-one would wish to suggest that the most heavily taxed countries are generally inefficient but the fact remains that some other governments can offer as much while demanding less. On the basis of this argument we can eliminate (on the figures for 1966) the countries in which the administrations seem to be too expensive: viz.

Sweden	46·9%
France	44·8%
W. Germany	40·2%
Norway	40·1%

The Netherlands, with 39·5%, only just escape elimination and W. Germany and Norway may be thought to have been unlucky to have missed by so small a margin. However, the United Kingdom, with 36·2%, is so far clear. Countries still in the running are:

Belgium	Ireland
Canada	Netherlands
Finland	South Africa
Greece	United Kingdom
Israel	USA

We have now to apply the test of literacy. Britain and Ireland

claim that 100% of their citizens are literate, meaning no doubt
that they all attended school. While we may reject this claim,
regarding the Canadian return (98·7) as more realistic and the
American return (97·6) as probably correct, the countries
which fall below 95% must be thought to have less than an
acceptable standard in education. On this basis we have to exclude Israel (with 88%), Greece (with 82·3) and South Africa
(with 100% for Europeans but only 85% for Africans). We
should also have had to exclude some other countries, like
Portugal (90% literate), had they not been excluded already on
other grounds.

It is logical to consider next the question of crime and
punishment. We can fairly assume, to begin with, that the
outstandingly efficient countries are those in which order is
more easily maintained. The basic figure for comparison is the
number of crimes committed each year per 100,000 of population. The 1967 figure for indictable offences known to the
police in Britain (1,207,354 or 2,222 per 100,000 of the population) is a great deal too high but this may result, in part, from
the police being too few. With only one policeman per 554
people, the British might reasonably expect to have more crime
then the Irish, whose police are maintained in the proportion of
1 to 441. But Canada, with one policeman to 662, has a crime
index of 4,183·4 – nearly double that of Britain and more than
three times that of the Netherlands where the police force
numbers only 1 in 836. The Royal Canadian Mounted Police
have a well-deserved reputation for getting their man but the
fact remains that they have to do this too often. Canada has thus
to drop out of the semi-finals, leaving us to consider the prison
population in each of the countries on the short list. To have, on
an average day, one person in prison out of 500 might be
thought not unreasonable – even though Ireland in 1967 had a
proportion of one to 3,641 – but the American figure of one to

488 is too much; and even that is superior to Belgium whose
year-end figure (for 1965) was one in 364. The semi-finalists are
therefore:

Finland	Netherlands
Ireland	United Kingdom

All these countries have a high level of administrative competence and it would be appropriate to apply to all of them a
further test of economy in effort. What proportion of administrative staff to working population was needed to produce
the ordered and sensible society which each one of them must
possess? There are difficulties here of definition, unfortunately,
but the proportion – excluding municipal staff – comes to
much the same in each case: 1 in 31 (Britain), 1 in 33 (Ireland),
1 in 34 (Finland) and 1 in 34 (Netherlands). Britain loses here by
comparison with the others but the margin is small and it might
seem fairer to apply another and more decisive test. For what
number of workers was one day in the year lost as a result of
industrial dispute? To make the competition doubly fair we
have taken a ten-year period and ascertained the average. The
figures which result are these:

Netherlands	58
Finland	8
United Kingdom	6
Ireland	3

Had the final contest produced a closer result we should
have applied one further test: the number of psychiatric
patients per 1,000 of the population. This gives a fair indication
of mental stress and the prevalence of neuroses. This would
equally have eliminated Ireland, where the figure would have
been 7·3 as compared with Britain's 4·6, Finland's 3·6 and the
Netherlands 2·3. Were we to have brought in the 1967 un-

employment figures they would have reinforced our conclusion, the Netherlands having the lowest figure (1·7 per
cent) followed by Finland and Britain (2·1 per cent) and Ireland
(5·9 per cent). The result of the contest is a victory, therefore,
for the Netherlands with Finland as a very creditable second.

On the basis of these calculations, the Netherlands Government is awarded the Parkinson Prize, and Finland is highly
commended. Within the limits of this inquiry there can be no
doubt that substantial justice has been done. While publishing
these results, however, the author has to qualify them in three
respects. In the first place, the bases of comparison are not, of
necessity, ideal. The statistics used are those available in a
sufficiently similar form and were chosen for that reason.
Efficiency might be measured in a number of other ways, given
a sufficient research team employed over a sufficient period of
time. The recurring difficulty is one of definition. What is a
policeman for statistical purposes and what is a psychiatric
patient? Prison warders may count as police in one country,
and lunatics in another may include all who have ever been
treated for a mental complaint. Any absolutely accurate comparison would, therefore, involve a large team in years of
inquiry and analysis. All one could claim at this stage, with any
scientific finality, is that national efficiency *can* be measured.
It is clear, moreover, that the example of the more efficient
might be studied with advantage by the rest. If our statesmen
should wish to argue that democracies are more competent
than, say, dictatorships, they must produce some form of
proof. The mere statement of preference is not enough. We
need to devise, develop and improve an acceptable basis of
comparison, known and respected throughout the world. After
merely months of effort the author would not claim to have
done more than prove that this is possible and suggest that it
should be done.

In the second place, there is a significant contrast between the size of many of the countries we have listed. The Netherlands have a population of only twelve and a half million, Finland a population of less than five, the one to be compared with Pennsylvania and the other with Missouri. There may be grounds for suspecting that units of that size are more efficient in the nature of things; a useful conclusion in itself. It is also possible that some States in USA might prove to be more competent than others and far more competent than the Union as a whole. While there can be no exact comparison between States which are wholly independent and others which form part of a Federation, the fact remains that the latter may have a local standard of efficiency which might bring them higher in some respects than their national level. Tasmania and Utah may thus deserve more attention than the author has so far been able to spare them. Incidental to this question of scale, it should be observed at this point that the Netherlands, smaller than New York State, have always formed a federation, not a unitary state, and that they can still boast a form of monarchy.

In the third place, we must remember that competence is not the only virtue a people may claim. Countries in which hygiene is poor and punctuality unknown may excel, for all we know, in other ways. Great art or music may flourish under a bungling administration and the most illiterate people may turn out to be athletic, pious and brave. For a place to have bred St Francis or Beethoven might be thought sufficient without its having to install main drainage as well. If our present emphasis is upon competence it is because that humdrum virtue is at least roughly measurable. Other qualities, more valuable perhaps in themselves, are largely a matter of opinion. Who could attempt to assess, for example, the standards of scholarship? Nobel prizes can be counted but who could say what they may signify? The number of students attending places of higher education might be ascertained, but what could the figures prove? The standard at graduation in College Z may equal the standard of entry at College A. Nor are we sure that the graduate engineer is better trained than the apprentice. There are all sorts of qualities which people may possess, not the less real for being statistically unprovable. Countries eliminated in the early stages of the present contest may be superb, for all we know, in other respects. It is not the author's intention to suggest that efficiency is all.

Having conceded so much to the losers, one must end, nevertheless, with a final word of congratulation to the people who have won. It might have been our fate to bestow the award on people known only for their honesty and hard work or people lacking any other sort of achievement. The Dutch, however, can point to something more than a sensible administration. Theirs is the land of Vermeer and Rembrandt, Tromp and De Ruyter, Grotius and Descartes. They have made their contribution in architecture and painting, in discovery and war. For the numbers of their population, they have produced as much talent as any people, perhaps, in modern times. If they have made for themselves an ordered society and a sound economy, it is not because they were endowed from the outset with material resources and impregnable frontiers. Much of their land they have won from the sea, most of their trade they have won from their neighbours and all of their industry they have created for themselves. That they should prove competent need surprise no-one, for no incompetent folk in their situation could even have survived. As for Finland, the land of Sibelius, which gained second place, this country has at least a comparable achievement in its survival. For a people to have retained their independence on the very doorstep of Tsarist and Soviet Russia is a feat of courage as well as of competence. Without efficiency they could not be where they are and as undaunted as they remain. Dutch and Finns alike, then, have special problems of their own which they have tackled with resolution. Perhaps we should conclude that the highest efficiency is characteristic of people to whom danger is never remote.

Chapter 3

BUCKMASTERSHIP

The desk of a recent President of the United States was said to be adorned by a framed notice saying 'THE BUCK STOPS HERE.' This assumption of responsibility was, no doubt, generally admired but the origin of the expression is not generally known. According to the *Concise Oxford Dictionary*, a buck is an article placed as a reminder before a player whose turn it is to deal at Poker. But what *was* the object used for this purpose?

The Random House Dictionary would have it that a buckhorn knife was most commonly used. Shifted privily, it could thus transfer the responsibility to someone else, the process being called 'Passing the Buck'. The phrase, if not the idea, had its origin in the United States but has since become current in Britain and the Commonwealth. It means, let us agree, that the buck-passer shifts the responsibility to another person, together with all the possible blame for having given the wrong answer. This is, of course, a common practice in the over-organized world of today.

In any large organization, business as well as public, the buck can be passed in three directions: [1] downwards, [2] sideways, and [3] upwards. The buck-passing executive accompanies his action by a telephone call, his words chosen, respectively, as follows:

(1) 'That you, Underleigh? Buckmaster here. I am sending you back the file on the Perilous Project as put forward by Morgan Merlin. I feel that this should be dealt with by you. I do not say that you were wrong to send it forward in the first place but I do know that the Chief likes to see signs of initiative at every level. So make your own decision and let me know afterwards what you have done. I have every confidence in your judgement.'

(2) 'That you, Longstop? Brian Buckmaster here. I am sending you the file on the Morgan Merlin affair, which has come to my office in error. You will realize when you glance at it that we in this Department are not in any way involved. The questions which arise are technical and legal but not administrative. We are always most careful not to trespass on your territory and this is certainly best left to the experts. It is good to have a man of your knowledge and experience – I shouldn't, myself, know the first thing about it. Over to you and the best of luck.'

(3) 'That you, Miss Cushion? Assistant Under Secretary here. I am sending Sir Arthur the file on the Merlin Project. He will realize, when he sees my minute, that the decision is one I cannot make myself. The political and financial implications are a bit beyond me and I hardly think my filing cabinet should contain a document with so high a security classification. I know that Sir Arthur will know how to deal with it.'

Nearly every file that comes to Buckmaster is thus neatly passed to someone else, being always too important (or else too trivial) for him. When the file has been rejected by every other department and when his own chief has told him to deal with it personally, he finally writes a minute on these lines:

This crucial matter would seem to admit of two possible solutions, A and B. In favour of A there are the following cogent arguments: (*i*) ... (*ii*) ... (*iii*) ... and (*iv*) ... *As against that*, there are the following reasons for preferring B:
(*i*) ... (*ii*) ... (*iii*) ... and (*iv*) ...
I suggest that the Minister should decide.

Faced with such a minute one politician wrote 'I agree' in the margin, subsequently explaining that he concurred in the view that the two alternatives were indeed those that had been defined.

Buckmastership is not, let us emphasize, confined to the Civil Service, being endemic to every large organization. It is more particularly characteristic, however, of the pyramid-type structure in which the incoming problem is first considered at the lowest level. There is in that hierarchy a further tendency to ratify a low-level decision by a high-ranking signature. This process begins with Bottomley, to whom the matter is first referred. However inexperienced and junior, he perceives that the answer to the application must be either 'Yes' or 'No'. Fearing that 'Yes' may involve him in a lot of extra work, he suggests the answer 'No'. He does this lightheartedly because the final decision must be taken, as he knows, on a higher level. The chances are that Underleigh will reverse his recommendation on principle, merely to keep him in his place, and that he in turn will be over-ruled by someone else. All Bottomley has done (he supposes) is to waft the thing on its way. But Underleigh is distracted that day, as it happens, by something else and fails to form an opinion of any sort. He absently signifies rejection and passes the file on to Middlebloke, knowing of course that the final decision will not be his. Middlebloke, with other things on his mind, absent-mindedly confirms the 'No' before passing the file to Upperman. But Upperman has come to rely upon Middlebloke, whose ability has been tested over the years. He submits a formally negative reply to Topdog for signature. It is one of the weaknesses, however, of the pyramid process that nearly everything converges on Topdog's desk. He can do no more than glance at the papers he has to sign, relying on Upperman to see that each decision is the right one. Out goes the reply and the answer is 'No'. The fact that the answer has taken six weeks to produce might convince a naïve applicant that the proposal has been the subject all that time of grave deliberation in solemn conclave. It is the sad fact, on the contrary, that it has never been discussed at all.

What is wrong with the paper-passing process is that everyone relies upon everyone else. The man at the bottom assumes that the men at the top know best. Frantically busy, the men at the top assume that the whole subject has been thoroughly investigated by the men at the bottom, who alone have time to work on it. In the imaginary case described, any one man would have done better by himself than the five did between them, as he would at least have known that the decision was to be his. As things were, each executive assumed that the work would be done or had been done on another level, whereas no work had been done by anyone. And this, believe it or not, is an accurate picture of what can actually happen, especially when the final answer is negative. A positive decision is less easily reached because the question may then arise of what further action should be taken by whom, 'Yes' being seldom enough in itself.

It would be wrong, of course, to assume that no bucks are passed in the home and among the family. The day may begin with mother asking father to switch on the electric fire and may end with father asking mother whether she has put the cat out. In the meantime little Bobby has persuaded his older sister,

Margaret, to do his homework for him, while Margaret has cajoled Jeremy into pumping up her rear bicycle tyre. We all agree, therefore, that responsibility should be thus decentralized and so made to devolve upon someone else. There is a contrast, however, with public life in that laziness in the home can never be hidden. Where someone fails to do his share it is immediately obvious and becomes a subject for comment. Nor is the smaller organization very different from the family, its officials being too few to be faceless. As we pass, however, to larger administrative units we find that the scope for paper-passing and decision-dodging becomes progressively larger; which is one reason, among others, why the smaller organization is often the more efficient.

A Court appointment still in existence is the Mastership of the Queen's Buckhounds. Whether the Master was ever responsible for training the Civil Service is a matter of doubt among historians. That his post is now a sinecure is manifest, for our public officials seem to require no instruction in the buck-passing art. If we accept the fiction, however, that the Mastership is still a key post in our administration, we have the chance to accord it some recognition. Whenever the Whitehall Buck has been passed with particular dexterity the Leader of the Opposition might move that the salary attached in the Buckhound Mastership should be increased by (say) five shillings a year. Let it still be our boast that we give credit where credit is due.

And for the future? A time may come when an effective decentralization – with provincial Parliaments established in such cities as Edinburgh, Cardiff, Winchester and York – will have so revolutionized our administration that the old customs of Whitehall will be forgotten. Then that old Inn sign 'THE PASSING BUCK' will be a mystery, perhaps, to young people who have never heard the expression in common use.

Chapter 4

LA RONDE

Beatrice and Sidney Webb used to divide their friends into Categories *A* and *B*: the *A*s being aristocratic, anarchic or artistic; the more reliable *B*s being bourgeois, bureaucratic or benevolent. Such a division of mankind has been observable, in fact, from an early period of history. The Jews had their Pharisees and Sadducees, the Chinese their Taoists and Confucians. In Byzantium there were the blues and the greens, led respectively by landowners and merchants. As for Britain and the United States, the Cavaliers and Roundheads crossed the Atlantic and largely destroyed each other in the American Civil War.

In general the *A* traditions are based upon agriculture and breeding, the *A* loyalties and the *A* preferences are for ritual, colour, dancing, music and sport. The *B* traditions are based upon business and industry, the *B* loyalties are to urban institutions and sectarian groups, and the *B* preferences are for economy, order, sobriety, saving and prayer. When a motor coach is held up by hounds and horsemen, the passengers mostly reveal their outlook by exclaiming either [*A*] 'Look – there's the Princess!' or [*B*] 'What in heaven's name are we waiting for?'

We know, in practice, that no sane person is completely *A* or *B*. In so far as rabid extremists have existed on either side, we are descended from both. In all of us there mingles uneasily the epicurean and stoic, the Cavalier and Roundhead, the Tory and Whig, the moralist and rake. Granted this mixture, however, we mostly end in one camp or the other and are more committed to it as time goes by.

The *A* and *B* categories are not founded upon wealth or

poverty but upon differing kinds of motivation. On the *A* side, the individual or family seeks to rise in terms of status or rank, the ladder being traditionally military. On the *B* side, the individual or family seeks to rise in terms of piety and wealth, the ladder being essentially economic.

When we compare these two types of motivation we are foolish if we claim a general superiority of one over the other. For the need for a balance between *A* and *B* is manifest. Different situations call for different virtues, those of the church-warden being distinct from those of the fighter pilot. Our country has been fortunate in having both, the Tory squire being prominent at one moment, the Methodist merchant at the next. For one side to destroy the other would be, in all likelihood, a form of national suicide.

Whereas society is divided vertically by the line which separates *A* from *B*, it is divided horizontally by the gradations of success and failure. People can thus be grouped under the headings of the Desperate, the Passive, the Collectively Ambitious, the Ambitious and (finally) the Privileged. These levels are associated with income, but the collectively ambitious, striving to improve the position of a group, are not poorer, of necessity, than the personally ambitious, striving to improve the position of themselves.

The collectively active folk on the *A* side are typified by the accountants or surveyors who seek to emphasize the respectability of their professional association. The collectively active people on the *B* side are eager, by contrast, to raise the wage level of the boiler fitters or stevedores. More personally ambitious is the accountant who makes himself a director or the fitter who makes himself a member of parliament. A diagram representing our social structure, as so far described, might look like two ladders, *A* and *B*, placed side by side and ascending from despair to privilege.

But the picture is incomplete if it omits two other related tendencies. For people or families who have climbed up ladder *B* very often reveal a belated preference for the top of ladder *A*. The grandson of the successful puritan goes to Eton and Trinity. And this – as the grandfather may growl from his deathbed – is the first step towards that financial ruin which will plunge a later generation into the depths of despair. To fight their way out of the ranks of the desperate, a still later generation will amost certainly have to revert from *A* to *B*.

The effect of these two tendencies (*B* to *A* at the top, *A* to *B* at the bottom) is to turn the two ladders into a circle, as in Figure 1. From the bottom people can climb on either side of

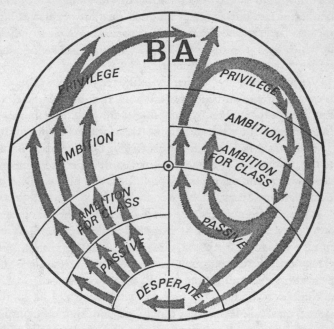

Fig. 1

the central dividing line. From barrow-boy [B] the cunning or lucky X will rise to privilege as a mail-order millionaire, with a grandson [A] in the Brigade of Guards. From private soldier [A] the brave and energetic Y will rise to privilege [A] as lieutenant-colonel D S O and J P.

We should notice, however, that the general movement is clockwise. We should also observe that those ascending on the A side rise more rapidly if they keep to the left and skirt the B side of society. The ranker colonel may thus play the stock market or marry the banker's daughter; and in practice will need to do both. On the B side a path to the right of the average would be followed by a business man of the more cautious sort, his mind already A-conditioned. He would thus move neither as fast nor as far as his rival on the speculative and spectacular left. The more dynamic societies are clearly those in which the forces of ambition and extravagance swing most widely towards the circumference.

We must note, finally, that the existence of ruin and despair is essential to the movement as a whole. If noblemen failed to impoverish themselves by gambling there would be no room in Privilege [A] for the ambitious [A] or for the Privileged [B]. The disaster which befalls the aristocrat, hurling his children to the depths, is at once the necessary complement to someone else's success and the necessary preliminary to his own descendant's later recovery.

It must be obvious that the circle is really a wheel. It generates power at the centre by the application of forces which are most effective near the circumference. For maximum efficiency each section but the lowest must offer a resistance and exact a price for admission. It must never, on the other hand, exclude everybody. The door must be there or the whole system must fail. It is at least equally obvious that momentum is increased by the dissipation of the dissolute and the folly of the fool. Without extravagance, gambling, drink and sex, Privilege [A] would be closed; and the closing of any one section must bring the whole movement to a halt. Where this happens the forces of pent-up ambition will eventually cause an explosion.

Where the opposite conditions prevail, with all doors flung wide open to uncompetitive entry, the forces may be active but the wheel is idle. The first step towards losing effective power is to give education away too easily, with high school for everyone and college for all. The path to promotion is thus dramatically opened but as much to the idle as to the energetic. All can move into the clerical levels of industry, but higher wages go to the few who remain on the factory floor. All sense of direction is lost and everything comes to a standstill. There are, in fact, danger limits in either direction. Exactly where the limits are might be difficult to decide, but great achievements in the past were seldom associated with either stagnation or chaos.

In England the areas associated with A and B are geographically distinct. To map them, we first need to superimpose the Industrial Revolution on the Civil War (Figure 2). The Roundheads' country lay to the south and east and it was their capture of Liverpool that split the Cavaliers' territory into two parts, the north and the west. The Industrial Revolution took place mainly in what had been Roundhead country, with a few outlying areas which fell to Methodism. That these maps are still relevant might be confirmed by the addition of further diagrams illustrating trade union membership and the location of co-operative stores.

In so far as the social structure diagram (Figure 1) can be applied to the map (Figure 2), the result would resemble Figure 3. Here the centre line (with the south-east at the top) connects London and Liverpool. To be more precise, it runs from Hastings to Mad Freshfield Wharf, splitting London between the West End and the City, and indeed splitting the Houses of Parliament between the Commons and the Lords.

Fig. 2

Central to the whole system – as must by now be obvious –
is the village of Edgcote in Northamptonshire. At the bottom
of the map is the Liverpolitan Region of Despair, divided between the Desperate [A] of Birkenhead and the Desperate [B]
of Warrington or Salford. Cambridge is, of course, central to
Ambition [B] and Oxford, with a majority of the public
schools, may epitomise Ambition [A]. East of the centre line,
the Desperate [B] from Manchester or the formerly passive
from Sheffield may break, with an effort, into the more ambitious counties of Nottingham or Leicestershire. They may
thus graduate from the hunting field to Cambridge, and so
storm into London via Liverpool Street.

After making a fortune, a family of this origin may well
achieve Privilege [B] in Norfolk or Kent; or even, better still,
on the Essex–Suffolk border. But Colchester, however attractive, is all too far from Windsor Castle. When the lure of

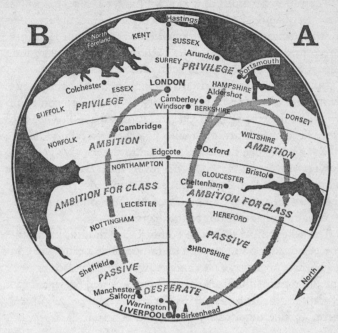

Fig. 3

Privilege [A] becomes impossible to resist, the family will move Westwards by way of Knightsbridge and find a new home near Arundel.

Meanwhile, other families from passive Shropshire or Hereford have begun their march on Cheltenham. Graduating from Oxford, some head for Whitehall or Portland Place. Graduating from Sandhurst or Greenwich, others head for Aldershot, Camberley, or Portsmouth. They mostly end in the very heart of Privilege [A], which is, of course, Berkshire; but other military families fall back, defeated, on Gloucester or the Bristol Channel.

There are exceptions, as we know, but the general tendencies are, surely, undeniable. Army officers seldom come from industrial Lancashire and millionaires as rarely from Hereford, Brecon or feudal Dorset. The patterns of success have long been established and are sufficiently known.

But are the patterns eternal? The aim of the Labour party is avowedly to create a classless society. Were this to come into existence, the barrier between Ambition [B] and Privilege [B] would become unsurmountable. To achieve wealth would be all but impossible, nor would its achievement give access to power. Movement on the higher levels from B to A would be more than balanced by the movement from A to B. With the abolition, moreover, of the Desperate, the momentum would be equally lost at the foot of the diagram.

The wheel must therefore come to a standstill, its motive power gone. Socialists would describe this as a calm and contented state of affairs. Calm and serenity might indeed prevail, but all pressure indicators would have flickered down to zero. Perhaps for the first time, a Labour prime minister might feel, therefore, that the situation was under control.

Chapter 5

LORDS AND LACKEYS

In an excellent book entitled *Management and Machiavelli* (1967) Mr Anthony Jay reminds us that the top executives of any large organization – whether political, industrial, military or religious – can be classed either as barons or courtiers. A medieval king had a rather uncertain control over his more powerful nobles, to whom whole provinces might owe their primary allegiance. More immediately under his eye, however, were the experts to whom he must turn for advice; the bishops, bankers, judges and generals who formed his actual retinue. The courtier was important through having access to the King and retained his importance for just so long as the King thought him useful. The baron was important in himself – his strength based on an actual territory – but his access to the King was only occasional. Under a weak rule the barons were all-important, the King merely playing off one against another. Under a strong rule, the courtiers were more active and the barons more subdued. Personalities apart, an expedition against another kingdom – or better still, a crusade – would centralize power at headquarters, while the threat of attack would give new importance to the barons on the threatened frontier. And what was true of the Middle Ages has remained true ever since. Feudal kingdoms have given place to industrial combines but the basic facts are the same. The courtiers are the heads of production, marketing, advertising and finance. The barons are the managers of the several plants. And while the courtier's success is measured by the favour which is shown him by the Managing Director, the baron's success is to be judged by the percentage yield on the capital invested in his division. These are among the immutable facts of administration, as true today as at the time of the Norman Conquest. The courtiers have always wanted to centralize and the barons have always fought for their autonomy. The conflict between them is in the nature of things and is not to be resolved by any sudden glimpse of eternal truth.

If there is a feature of the medieval court which the modern head office fails to reproduce, it is the ancient office of Fool or Jester. It was the Fool's privilege and duty to put forward another point of view, neither that of the Establishment nor that of the group currently out of favour. If the traditions of his office mean anything, the official Jester would seem to have been at least as clever as any other official. There was no need to take his advice seriously but neither was there much excuse for taking offence at anything he said. To talk out of turn was, after all, what he was paid to do. There is reason to think that he served a useful purpose and there is even some reason to suspect that he might be useful now. Or is his modern counterpart the industrial psychologist? The idea of the official Fool is at least worthy of study, for there is otherwise no way of pricking the bladders of self-satisfaction. It is when the chorus of mutual praise reaches its climax that someone is needed to say 'Rubbish!' It is true that anyone may say that now, but not without danger of making enemies. The Fool was privileged, remember, and allowed a sort of diplomatic immunity. Here is an instance of a useful office unfilled. A parallel office which has recently come to life again is that of the King's Confessor; a shadowy figure who may never have lacked influence. He has reappeared as the psycho-analyst, the man to whom the Chairman of the Board may turn for spiritual guidance. Apart, then, from the Fool, the head office of today is much like the court of yesterday, and especially so in its general agreement on the need to centralize.

The urge to centralize authority in one headquarters has always been present in every large organization. Personal interests apart, moreover, there are some solid arguments for centralization. Only the men at the centre, it can be urged, have the whole picture. In defending medieval Britain the Prince Bishop of Durham and the Duke of Northumberland might be thought to have an obsession with the Scots. On the Marches of Wales no one could talk about anything but Welsh marauders. The barons of the Cinque Ports had as narrow an outlook, mind you, with their fixation about piracy. Only at court was it possible to compare these different reports and decide where the real danger (if any) was to be feared. On the basis of this decision, resources might be sensibly allocated and diplomacy used where troops might be lacking. The top-level decision has also the merit of finality. If all these barons were called together, they would argue for ever, back-biting, mudslinging and challenging each other to mortal combat. What the situation called for was a crisp, clear order from the Earl Marshal beginning (more or less) with the words, 'I am commanded by His Majesty . . .', and ending, 'Fail at your peril!' A modern cabinet decision is supposed to have the same effect and the industrial equivalent is a letter signed by the Chairman of the Board of Directors. Having reviewed the whole situation the Board has decided to close the branch at Basingstoke and expand the factory at Newcastle-on-Tyne. All the northern units of production will be directed from a new divisional office at York and a special export department will be set up near Canterbury. The policy has been decided and the argument is over. Our target is to increase production by $12\frac{1}{2}\%$ over the next two years. 'Fail at your peril!'

As unvarying through the centuries is the reaction from the fringes of the organization. The Lords Marcher tell each other that these chaps in London are completely out of touch. It is all very well to issue directions but these chairborne types are unaware of the facts. The line of march they indicate is not cavalry country at all. And what about the forage? As for the road they seem to rely upon, that ceased to exist last winter. The fact is that you need local knowledge and it has to be up-to-date.

The political situation, moreover, is changing the whole time. Of the chiefs they want us to capture one is now on our side, and the other is dead. The impatience of the man-on-the-spot with the armchair strategist is paralleled today in the reaction of the branch manager to the head office policy. The advertisements compiled in London will be ineffective in Dundee and the goods packaged for sale in Chelsea will remain unsold in Belfast. And why, for heaven's sake, plan this extension to the No. 3 Plant? We cannot recruit the labour for the machines we already have! As for this apprenticeship scheme, with classes in engineering and economics, Head Office fail to realize that apprentices are unobtainable in this area. All this correspondence from London is unrealistic. It would be better if these pundits would come and look at the situation for themselves. As things are, we are (frankly) fed up!

Here, then, are the two basic points of view. And the men-on-the-spot have tended, until fairly recently, to have their own way. For the central government, however strong, has lacked, throughout history, the means of making its rule effective. There might be the will to govern but the letters took too long to arrive. And as soon as the oceanic empires were founded (whether political or commercial) the lines of communication were stretched to an impossible length. With six months spent in delivering the letter and six months more in awaiting the reply, the distant proconsul held all the cards. By the mere device of asking for clarification he could postpone action for a year, at the end of which time a changing situation would have made the policy inapplicable. For centuries the central administration wrestled with this most intractable of problems, demanding information and issuing orders but always with the sensation of one who seeks to control a jelly-fish by means of an elastic lead. With obvious reluctance the imperial rulers and commercial directors had had to concede viceregal powers to men whose ability might be great but whose loyalty was doubtful. Their position at head office has been one in which they could almost die of frustration. For the disobedient baron is often impossible to replace and it is not every Truman who dares fire his MacArthur. Until quite recently the means of control simply did not exist.

The whole situation began to change quickly as from about 1870. There came successively the telegraph, the pulp-paper (for duplication), the telephone, the steamship and the car. There followed the teleprinter, the radio, the aircraft and the jet. Quite abruptly, the centre of each empire – whether political or commercial – was given the means of asserting its power. Kings, presidents and directors were suddenly able to extract the fullest information, issue the most precise instructions and expect the most abject obedience, all in a matter not of days but hours. Viceroys became agents, ambassadors became messengers and managers became executives. By 1900, and still more by 1950, the barons were a shadow of their former selves, and the courtiers were everywhere in the ascendant. As if to clinch matters, the head office acquired a computer – a crystal ball in which the whole organization can be seen at a glance. 'Magic mirror on the wall, who's the cleverest of all?' The witchcraft of today will give the answer in a flash with statistical proof to follow. The eyes of the Lord are upon the modern manager and he refers every decision to one above. At any hour he can be summoned to heaven and made to give an account of his stewardship. At any moment an archangel may appear in his office and ask to see the accounts. The baron of today tends to be very much on the leash.

Centralization is the current fashion and each merger makes the trend more absolute. It becomes obvious, however, that there are drawbacks in this process which the central administrators did not at first foresee. Control depends upon information and the first demand from head office is for accounts and statistics, returns and reports. The result is that the paper flows in from a widespread empire, each babbling brook going to swell what ends as a shining river. Paper breeds, as we have to realize, and statistical returns become more elaborate each year. Head office is finally swamped with information, whole departments being engaged merely in filing it away. Floors are stacked with steel cabinets and clerks are absorbed in a lifework of cross-reference. The central sorcerer demanded facts and the sorcerer's apprentice has started a process by which facts in quadruplicate arrive by the bucketful. So far from anyone looking at the paper, people have barely the time to put each document in the right folder. Each office is swamped in a foaming torrent of information, no one knowing how to turn off the tap. Any room left empty with a name on the door would be packed solid in two years with the accumulated weight of correspondence. Unwary executives drown helplessly in the paper flood, while self-preservation is all that many others can claim to have achieved.

Converse of the paper flood is the problem of the shortening day. Head offices, whether governmental or industrial, tend to be placed in larger cities, which have become unfit for habitation. Executives, who usually measure their status in terms of distance from the centre, live most of them, therefore, beyond the fringe. Rising admittedly before daybreak, they do well to be at their desks by 10.0. To reach home again, moreover, by 7.0, they need to be out of the office by 4.0. With a lunch interval from 12.0 to 2.0, their day's toil amounts thus to about four hours in all. The wider and more complex the spider's web, the more business reaches head office and the less time is available in which to deal with it. The wrong decisions are made too late and quite urgent problems are swamped in trivialities and tea. Supreme in this sense of futility is the Palace of Westminster where mere congestion of business brings everything to a standstill. In the departments of Whitehall a pyramid structure of responsibility brings each major decision to the summit level at which nobody has the time to study it. In industry a similar hierarchy works for as short a day to produce almost as small a result. In every large head office we see today the results of over-centralization taken to the point of lunacy.

Concentration of power at the centre does more than create chaos where all the lines converge. Carried to excess, it also causes frustration at the circumference from where they start. It is from among the divisional chiefs that the future Managing Director should be chosen, for it is only in an executive (rather than advisory) position that a man is tested on the basis of results as contrasted with opinions. But little is either proved or learnt in a branch office which merely sorts the mail and asks for guidance. The result is that morale suffers and executives resign, those left being of uncertain quality and of little experience. In the absence of men with a reputation made in a responsible post, the Board will look to head office for its next chief executive. But departmental heads are seldom ideal candidates for further promotion. Their knowledge is specialized and they are unused to a responsibility that is not shared with others. Least of all are they the sort of men who could restore the morale of the branch offices. Over the past years they have provided technical advice rather than leadership. No one of these elderly men is likely to spring into action at the eleventh hour, belatedly proving himself a ball of fire. Unless new talent can be brought in from outside the company may be in for a very dull period indeed. Over-centralization may lead to no immediate disaster; but there is a final penalty and the time will come when it has to be paid.

The current trend is towards over-centralization but the reaction against it has already begun. In the largest American industrial groups the several divisions are often given a free hand in everything but general policy and finance; and this is, surely, the example to follow. As against that, it would be wrong to think that there is a golden rule by which we can fix a midway point between excessive and insufficient control. John Stuart Mill urged that information should be centralized but that power should be distributed. That is a useful rule so far as it goes but there can be no formula which will fit every organization at every period of its history. The situation changes and our survival depends upon the speed with which we can re-deploy and reorganize. If there is a general principle, however, it would be that centralization is more needed when launching an offensive, decentralization when we are expecting the enemy's attack.

Chapter 6

PRINCIPALITIES AND POWERS

During the centuries of European expansion the Nation State was evolved as the normal political unit. This was mainly for purposes of war. France was unified for fear of England, Spain for fear of Islam, Great Britain for fear of Spain and Germany for fear of France. For aggressive war the nation state was the largest unit which would not fall apart through divergence of regional interests. For administrative efficiency the nation was often too large and for economic convenience it was usually too small. With Europe once more on the defensive against Asia, it is generally recognized that some reorganization is needed. The movement towards European unity – of which the European Economic Community is an expression – foreshadows a new Roman Empire with all the advantages that had to offer in terms of defence, free trade and internal peace. But this urge to unite as a continent is accompanied, quite logically, by a demand for provincial autonomy. For the smaller political sub-units (Bavaria, Normandy, Scotland) have all sacrificed something of their local pride to the idea of nationalism. They have traded their independence for protection, and still more, for a share in the national achievement. When the British Empire was at its height, the Scots had a very fair share in its prosperity; so fair a proportion that they were willing to regard themselves (for the moment) as British. There was in those days an imperial heritage in which they could take a pride, just as there had been in Spain, Austria, France and Germany. In the second half of the 20th Century, by contrast, the nation state has little to offer its provinces in return for their allegiance. They cannot be defended save as part of a far larger alliance and there are nowadays no spoils of conquest in which they can share. The nation state, useful still in some ways, is a more obvious encumbrance in others, halting trade on a network of frontiers and wasting time over a grossly over-centralized administration. There are efficient nation states like Finland, Denmark or Sweden but these are of merely provincial size with populations of about four to seven millions. Where the population exceeds ten millions there is a manifest case for decentralization; as in the Netherlands, where each province has its own governor as in USA. This is the intellectual background for the movements which are now becoming urgent in Scotland and Wales. We have begun to realize that the nation state of thirty to fifty millions is hopelessly incompetent, with a deadening effect on provincial culture and a drearily standardizing effect on social life. For all purposes of internal administration we want a government which is accessible and economic, administering an area which is culturally unified and reasonably small.

The corollary, therefore, to European unity is a new emphasis on provincial autonomy. This offers two tremendous advantages of a merely practical kind. In the first place our dreary arguments about socialism can be relegated to the provincial level. All the industries can thus be nationalized in one region, and all left to private enterprise in another. Problems of health and housing would never be discussed in Paris or Rome: where there would be time, therefore, to deal with matters which are genuinely national and international. Our present policy is to kill all initiative on the periphery and leave no time for business at the centre. A parliament in Edinburgh, comparable to that of Northern Ireland, would be the first step towards reversing this policy, and this is what the Scots have rightly begun to demand. What we forget, however, is that a concession to Scotland, in terms of autonomy, must also relieve the pressure at Westminster. Whatever is done for Scotland should be at least equally beneficial to England, as indeed to the British Isles as a whole. It also suggests the possibility of Eire rejoining England in a looser type of federation; a move which would be of tremendous benefit to peoples whose flint-and-steel relationship used to achieve so much in the fields of leadership, literature and thought.

In some muddled way our politicians have begun to realize that decentralization must come. Their response, however, is to talk of creating a dozen administrative authorities in England, each to co-ordinate the economic efforts of the county and county borough councils in a given area. The objections to such a system of bureaucratic constipation are threefold. In the first place, the regions would not be of the proper size, comparable with (say) Denmark or Scotland. In the second place, they would lack any tradition of autonomy or basis in sentiment. In the third place, they would add to the existing paralysis by imposing another level of officialdom between the citizen and the legislature. The functions of a provincial parliament, as in Belfast, are to supersede the central parliament in every matter in which other regions are not involved. The construction of a Channel tunnel is an international problem, properly debated at Paris and Westminster. The organization of comprehensive schools (and their subsequent abolition) is a local matter, properly dealt with at Cardiff or Edinburgh. What no one out of bedlam could propose is a system by which an educational policy agreed at Edinburgh has to be debated again in London. That way lies madness, as must be obvious to anyone of even average intelligence. Our administration is cumbersome enough as it is. To add to its costly complexity would be tantamount to suicide.

Any serious proposal for provincial decentralization must begin, manifestly, with the effective units which exist. Scotland and Wales are historic countries which are comparable in size to Austria and Switzerland and as potentially efficient as Denmark and Norway. Assuming their autonomy, our need is for English regions which would roughly correspond in size and local patriotism. No sane person would attempt to plan such a grouping without long and careful inquiry into local ideas, needs and prejudice. We have seen colonial 'federations' in South-East Asia, Africa and the West Indies, all planned for administrative convenience without regard to what people actually want; and we have seen them fall to pieces as quickly as they were formed. We must realize now, even if we had previously forgotten, that such groupings must be based on some sort of human reality, not merely upon a departmental memorandum. We are bound, therefore, to approach the regional idea with the greatest caution. Our first proposals may well come to nothing. That need not, however, deter us from proposing something. On the assumption that a start must be made somewhere, can we fairly suggest that England should have six major divisions, each with a population of from five to seven millions? Might we insist, further, that the frontier drawn should correspond to some reality in historic background and contemporary fact? On these principles, the task is not (at least initially) so difficult.

The principalities into which England would seem to fall most readily are, surely, Anglia, Lancastria, London, Mercia, Northumbria and Wessex. There are admittedly, a score of difficult problems. Should Monmouth be regarded as English or Welsh? Is Cheshire more allied with Lancashire or Shropshire. Is Cornwall part of Wessex, part of Wales, or a separate country like Guernsey or Jersey? Is there sufficient affinity between Norfolk and Lincolnshire, between both and Rutland? Should Gloucestershire fall within the boundaries of Mercia or Wessex? There is scope enough for inquiry and argument but the general areas indicated – North-East, North-West, Midlands, East and South – have each some kind of unity. It is true that Wessex might be thought to divide on a line between Somerset and Wiltshire, between Hampshire and Dorset, but the western division would be small in population and without Cornwall would be smaller still. It may be, therefore, that all to the south of the Thames and Severn should constitute a single region. At the other end of the country the original North-umbria extended either side of the Pennines and comprised both Yorkshire and Lancashire. The mere size of this aggregate is an obstacle to its exact revival, quite apart from any memory of past rivalries between white rose and red. These consider-ations point to a smaller Northumbria with its capital at York and a reduced Lancastria with its capital at Manchester. Win-chester might be the capital of Wessex, Peterborough that of Anglia and Birmingham that of Mercia. These, and perhaps other and newer centres, would revive the distinctive life of the provinces, leaving London pre-eminent but no longer in a class utterly by itself. Here is the sort of Britain from which Ireland might not for ever feel estranged. With Ireland itself reunited, the States of Britain might eventually number nine, central-ized only for a limited purpose and known above all for their diversity.

If any such reorganization is to succeed, breaking the log-jam at Westminster and ending the more irrelevant squabbles of the Left and Right, we can be sure of one thing; the groundwork must be done in the provinces. There are planners enough at Whitehall but this is something which must come from the grass-roots, as in Scotland and Wales. The response to Welsh Nationalism is an English Provincialism which will keep our Celtic neighbours within the bounds of what is practicable. For while their aspirations are justified, they must remember that the old insular type of nationalism is out of date, and that com-plete independence is no longer in vogue. Irish resentment against England, justifiable as it was at the time, led to absurd-ities of insularity which no other country should repeat. Schoolchildren in Ireland waste up to ten hours a week in studying a language which was revived (if not actually in-vented) so as to annoy the English: a language which they will never speak and which they will presently forget. To introduce *another* language into a slowly unifying Europe where lin-guistic barriers must somehow be demolished, is to handicap one's children, at the outset, in a highly competitive field. The Scots, as business men, would never make that mistake; the Welsh, just possibly, might. From the errors of extremism the English can save them, not by persuasion but by example. If Mercia is coming into existence on their doorstep, the Welsh will realize that their own degree of autonomy need be no more than is claimed by the parliament which meets at Birmingham.

Chapter 7

A GAME CALLED MONOPOLY

Were Britain ever to become effectively decentralized we should still have a national Parliament at Westminster in which two major parties would compete for office. Were this alternation to cease, one party being perpetually in power (as in Sweden), we should presumably have to draw up a new constitution and organize the country in some other way. For this

policy there is, of course, much to be said. After exporting our constitution (or something vaguely resembling it) to a whole series of fairly unhopeful satellites, we should at least entertain the world were we to admit, finally, that we had found it unworkable even in Britain.

Few politicians, however, are ready to make that damaging admission, and most would agree that Parliament must continue to exist. While it does so, the two parties must play a game modelled, apparently, on that of cricket; a game in which no innings can be prolonged for ever. This means that there must be, from time to time, a Labour Government committed to conquering the 'commanding heights' of industry, a cabinet intent on bringing about 'a substantial expansion of public ownership'. The Trades Union Congress voted in 1963 for the nationalization of road transport, the aircraft, steel and ship-building industries, and at least the major plants in electrical engineering. Progress towards this goal has been slow but the object remains to add perhaps another million to the two million already employed in the nationalized industries. Sooner or later we must expect to see more state monopolies created, more industries unified and brought under state ownership and other industries made subject to more and more government interference.

Considering this policy as publicly announced and as partly carried out, we need to be clear about two things. First, public ownership does not mean public control. The aircraft or shipping industry may be re-organized and bought with our money but we shall not control it. The Prime Minister will control it, deferring on wages policy to the Trades Unions concerned, but not otherwise answerable to anyone – save perhaps to the departed spirits of Beatrice and Sidney Webb. He will not be answerable to Parliament and it is dubious whether Ministers are compelled, or even entitled, to inform the House about nationalized industries except in the very broadest terms. Second, the process of nationalization is more or less irrevocable. The Conservatives tried timidly to go into reverse over steel and road haulage. But a process by which those or other industries should be nationalized and de-nationalized repeatedly is not technically possible. For who, to start with, will buy the shares? If we are to continue with two political parties and those the two we have, holding the views they do, we shall end with all industries more or less nationalized. For that is what the one party seems to want and the other cannot prevent or reverse. The only obvious alternative is to end our experiment in democracy, confessing that it has been a complete failure. Before we do that, however, there is one other possibility. Could we, by argument, show the people at large – including the Labour Party – that nationalization has gone far enough? It is arguable that this could be attempted and might even succeed: but on one condition, that we fight not against nationalization as such but against monopoly in that or any other form. This is the age of take-over bids and mergers, with great concentrations being formed of industrial power, sometimes (not always) backed by American capital. Dare we ask the business men of today to condemn monopoly? Dare we suggest that industrialists should declare their support for anything so old-fashioned as Free Trade? Shall we see, anyway, where the argument might lead us?

There are and have always been two basic methods of organizing commerce and industry. You can establish a monopoly or you can allow different firms to compete; and there are arguments to support either policy. Let us take, first, the case for monopoly. Some of the earlier monopolies were in kingship, in justice, in warfare, in heraldry, in religion and postal services. There was nothing inevitable about ending private enterprise in any of these directions. There could be different candidates for coronation. Lords could erect and make use of their own courts of law and their own gallows. There were rival Popes at one time and there are rival telegraph companies even now. It was agreed, nevertheless, that too many jurisdictions might lead to confusion. Rather later came monopolies in the East India Trade, the Slave Trade and many other types of business from the preparation of saltpetre to the development of Hudson's Bay. For all or most of these monopolies a case could be made out. With the 18th Century, however, came a revolt against monopoly in the name of free trade. The revolt spread from America to France and England,

and by the mid-19th Century the older monopolies were mostly abolished. The College of Arms and the Hudson's Bay Company were among the few survivors from the massacre. But new monopolies arose as the old ones vanished; the canals, turnpikes and railways being among the first of these, controlled from the outset by Act of Parliament. They at once exemplified and influenced a new age in which the trend was again towards monopoly; a trend which began with the railway and ended, for the moment, with space travel and the digital computer. There are things too large for the family firm to handle and an organization which expands for technical reasons, within the national framework, must end in a monopoly. For that and for most monopolies there is and has always been one strong argument; the argument of human safety. We vest the crown, the gallows, the artillery, the railway and the airline in a monopoly, explaining that the alternatives could be extremely dangerous. The big exception to the technical trend of the age is the horseless carriage or automobile, the expression of rampant individualism; and the resulting casualties are very heavy indeed. Individual freedom is inseparable from danger. The case against freedom is the case for safety.

Some monopolies are technically, financially, or even aesthetically, essential. But against all other monopolies there is a case and it rests upon the individual's freedom to choose. If the grocer is rude to his customers, they go to another grocer, and he is ruined; so grocers have to be polite – or more polite, anyway, than officials in a labour exchange. It was in defence of individual freedom that we thus abolished some monopolies in religion, education, politics and trade. In religion the case for monopoly had been that differing doctrines could lead to bloodshed, as often happened. As against that, every human institution develops a tendency to pursue its own and its members' interests. There is little difference in this respect between

the Law Society and Transport House, between the British
Medical Association and the Church of England, between
Winchester College and the Trades Union Congress. An institution exists to please itself and is controlled only by the
knowledge that the customer can go elsewhere. Monopoly
flourishes when there is nowhere else for the customer to go.

Where a monopoly exists it may be the result of deliberate
policy. It may as often be the result of an organization growing
to its optimum size within a national framework which may be
too small to be economic. But whatever their origin, monopolies exist and a group of them can easily dominate any
country's economy. Such a group may form an economic state
within the political state, one set of people having the money
and another set the government. This position, as we see in
Malaysia, is too unstable to last. Its instability can be remedied
in one of two ways; either the government takes over the
monopolies or the monopolies take over the government.
Were the steel industry such a monopoly we could allow (say)
Thomas and Baldwin to govern Britain, lending one of its
directors for the purpose. Or else we can nationalize Thomas
and Baldwin (as we have done) and so keep the Baldwin family
out of the cabinet. By nationalizing the steel industry, as the
Labour Party Ministers have done, we end the danger of
another Chamberlain coming from Birmingham Small Arms.
These are the broad alternatives offered by the Conservatives
and Socialists.

We cannot accept the Conservative solution because it has
manifestly failed. The Chamberlains could rule Birmingham
but to shift them from the City Council to Downing Street was
disastrous. So let us consider the socialist solution; nationalize!
It has, we have seen, a logical basis. Given the alternatives of
letting Birmingham run Whitehall, or allowing Whitehall to
run Birmingham, many of us might (after some hesitation)

C

choose the Whitehall regime as slightly the lesser of the two
evils. But the enthusiasts for nationalization see it rather as a
positive good, a source of happiness and gaiety. Whereas life
with the Market Snodborough Gas Company was dreary and
dull, the day of nationalization came and with it a new life for
everyone. The fitters and meter inspectors danced round the
gas-holders singing, 'Hey, nonny, nonny!' The householders
looked and still look upon the Ministry of Power with a senti-
mental affection for which history affords no previous example.
The old treadmill round of existence is finished and we can all
live happily ever after. We may not be quite certain about the
facts but this is, anyway, the theory. And even people whose
enthusiasm is less will argue that a nationalized industry should
give better service, offer higher wages and still show a profit.

What ground have they for believing this? Well, they can
point, first of all, to the traditions of service which have given
strength to some of the earliest institutions we nationalized: the
Navy, the Army, the Foreign Service or Trinity House. They
can point to other monopolies which have long served the
public interest: the Bank of England, the great hospitals,
the British Broadcasting Corporation, and, for that matter, the
Marylebone Cricket Club. Next, they can point to the suc-
cesses, such as they are, of British Rail, the National Coal
Board, the Electricity Council and the Atomic Energy Commission. They can show that monopolies have their merits.
They can argue, moreover, that nationalization and monopoly
do not necessarily go together. In the words of Mr Harold
Wilson, 'there is much to be said for the establishment of state-
owned competitive factories'. It is possible to show, nevertheless, that these arguments are fallacious.

Take, first of all, the traditions of service. Why should we
not endow our nationalized industries with all the proud
traditions we associate with the Brigade of Guards? Why

should not the primary schoolteachers have the same *esprit de corps* as the Royal Horse Artillery? Why should not the men of the Electricity Council hold themselves as proudly as the Royal Marines? All one can say is that they do not. If there is one nationalized monopoly with an old and proud tradition, it is the Royal Mail. The Post Office combines antiquity with royal patronage, a multiplicity of functions with an almost startling modernity of equipment. But the postmen as some fairly recent events have shown – are not quite as loyal to the Crown as they are to their own trade union. They will even query the nature of the mail they are told to distribute, just as dockers will query the destination of the shipments they handle. But that does not happen in the fighting services. The bomber pilot does not argue over the policy of saturation bombing. The officer of the guard does not dispute the need to defend the Bank of England. He merely carries out the orders he has received from an officer senior to him. It is dubious whether the Directors of the Postal Department can command a comparable obedience, even though their authority must be far greater than that of anyone (say) on the National Coal Board. There is little reason to suppose that the nationalized industries will look to Whale Island or Aldershot for their pattern of service. There is far more reason to fear that the armed services will take their tone from the coal mines. 'Strikes' where least expected have already taken place.

Defenders of monopoly point to the success of the nationalized industries. It is, however, a question whether their success has been proved. The mines were taken over by the National Coal Board in 1947 and first showed a small profit in 1962. The British Transport Commission control the railways and allied services which were nationalized in 1948 and have lost money steadily ever since, the losses of 1962 being three times those of 1958. We are told that nationalized industries are justified in making a loss. They are likened to the Post Office, which performs a public service and is not to be judged as a commercial undertaking. One may not be happy about this reasoning, but even accepting its validity, we may fairly conclude that there is a limit to the losses we can be expected to make good. We cannot indefinitely reduce the number of tax-paying industries, adding each year to the number of those that have to be supported by the rest. Lovers of nationalization may remind us at this point that it was the more or less bankrupt industries that were nationalized first. This is true, but *all* nationalized industries have a tendency to go bankrupt. Nor can it be otherwise, for the more an industry is identified with government the less chance it has to economize on salaries and wages. Why? Because every man discharged as redundant is a voter. Every additional man hired is also a voter. So that each party while in power wants to hire people. It postpones staff reduction, considering this a task better done by the Opposition when its turn for office comes. Under our system of parliamentary rule, the nationalized industries have thus a built-in trend towards bankruptcy. Nor is this trend one we can readily reverse.

What, finally, of this argument that nationalized industry can be set up in competition with private industry? This is an attractive proposal and our first instinct (as anti-monopolists) is to say, 'Good idea!' The BBC has been improved as a result of ITV competition, as most people would admit. It follows, therefore, that ITV, had it been the older organization, would have been improved by the setting up of the BBC as its rival. Where there are privately-owned monopolies, as in the motion picture industry, the setting up of publicly-owned organizations would be a means of encouraging the sort of competition we need. The theory is attractive. But what of the practice? Experience goes to suggest that the Government will not (and probably cannot) play fair. The fuel industries provide us with the classic test. We know now that even the Conservatives maintained a high duty on fuel oil in order to protect the interests of the National Coal Board. There was once a public admission to that effect. The government made up for this by half strangling the semi-nationalized segment of the motion picture industry. Why this sharp difference of attitude? Why should the wrong decision be made in each case? The explanation must be that the National Coal Board is now a part of the governmental structure, defended by the votes of its employees; whereas the film production vote is negligible. But if the Conservatives could not play fair, how much less can we expect from the Socialists – to whom the idea of competition was never sacred in the first place? Apparently fair competition between state-owned and privately-owned enterprise will always end as a monopoly again. The government, as employer, must protect its own – provided that there are votes involved – and cannot be trusted to act as referee.

The arguments for monopoly fall flat in every case. But there are also arguments against it. Some are too obvious to stress, but three are worth mentioning because they may be less familiar. The nationalized monopoly is eternally faced, first of all, with a dilemma. Is it a public service or is it a commercial undertaking? Is it part of the government or is it something distinct? Make it part of government and it will soon be run at a loss. The government cannot discharge its employees without losing votes. It *can* buy voters by distributing employment, or even sinecures, and this has often been done. Let us suppose, then, that the opposite policy is chosen. British Rail must stand on its own wheels. The National Coal Board must face the competition of oil fuel – and even the competition of imported coal. The first result is that public ownership ceases to involve even the pretence of public control. How could it be otherwise? Parliament can lay down the policy for railways, the Minister can control their freight rates and fares; but only on the assumption that a loss may, and probably will, result. The Minister cannot tell the directors to do this and that but *still* make a profit. Once we have decided that the management is to break even or show a modest return, we must leave the directors to do it in their own way.

In point of fact, our form of representative government does not even ensure that the question will be quickly decided. It offers us, rather, two competing policies. The conservatives will maintain that a nationalized industry must pay its way, or at least break even – penalizing free enterprise, if necessary, to make this possible – while the socialists will say that nationalized industries can make a loss and that the resulting deficit is of no consequence. In the long run the socialist policy will prevail. In fact it has begun to prevail already, with heavier losses being reported from year to year. Subsidies to nationalized industry have played no small part in handicapping our whole economy.

There is another disadvantage about a monopoly, whether nationalized or not. For the organization is apt to be handicapped by its mere size. Take as example one of the biggest mergers of our time, the one which led to the creation of the Ministry of Defence. Here we had three nationalized services, directly competing for manpower and money and indirectly competing for business. The government of the day decided upon a merger, imitating the Pentagon; where the same experiment has proved, incidentally, such a conspicuous failure. The cost of administration was vastly increased even in the first year. Our obvious and urgent need is for infantry, but we are missing the historic and famous regiments we have had the folly to disband. Instead of bayonets, we have clerks and filing systems, inter-office memoranda and cups of tea. Faced by an endless series of easily foreseeable emergencies, our policy has been to create a mammoth head office from which to control the movements of the troops we no longer possess and the cruisers we cannot even man. After another crisis or two, the next hysterical mob of rioters will be confronted by our last strategic reserve – probably the Yeomen of the Guard.

Apart from the question of their size, monopolies are not consistent with the form of representative government we have set up and are trying to retain. For once the monopolies have become identified with government, being merely the tools of official policy, the point is soon reached when the government comes to employ a majority of the electorate. This involves a change in the whole nature of both government and society. It means that state employees will be voting, in effect, on their own terms of service. At that point the choice lies between dictatorship and collapse.

Chapter 8
IMPERATIVE TENSE

Our ideas of authority derive from fatherhood and our terms of respect, in nearly every language, are the proof of it. Among human beings the young are dependent on their parents for a long time. The father is protector and teacher for so many years that the obedience he has to exact becomes habitual, creating in successive generations an attitude of respect towards

seniority as such. Such an attitude of deference is also traditionally displayed by the mother. With her, however, the father's relationship is more complex, for the survival of the kinship or tribe depends more upon its women than its men. In general, however, the father's rule extends over the whole group and the children's sense of subordination is firmly based upon common sense and tradition. Their attitude towards authority comprises three distinct elements: wonder, at the father's greater knowledge and skill; affection for one who is at least interested in ensuring the child's survival; and fear of punishment for disobedience. These three elements go to make up a sense of security. More particularly essential is the element of fear for if the child does not fear his father he can hardly suppose that his father will be feared by anyone else. And what is the protection worth of a man whom no one fears?

As the community grows larger the idea of fatherhood turns into kingship. From early times there have been two types of monarchy, the mobile and the static. Over a pastoral tribe, eternally on the move, the king is the leader, deciding the route, choosing the day and marking the camp site. Over an agricultural people the king is more of a priest, interceding with the gods so as to ensure the sunshine when it is wanted and the rain at the proper time. There is still room in the world for both types of authority. During World War II Lord Montgomery typified the leader in the field but Lord Alanbrooke was seldom ever seen, his authority looming behind the successive doors of the War Office. One was needed to give immediate direction, the other to intercede with higher authority for the army's proper share of the available manpower. Both types of authority have the same remote origin and both imply a mixture of reputation and power. Where the reputation has been lost, the power soon vanishes. Where the power has gone, the reputation cannot survive. The world is full of high-sounding titles from which all meaning has been drained. This has always been so, however. What is new is our present doubt as to whether authority itself can survive.

The first weakening of current authority resulted from the female revolution which took place in Britain and USA after about 1900. Skirts became trousers, women were to graduate and vote and the sexes were to be equal in nearly every way.

But the revolution ended in compromise and confusion. Allowed to be equal in the areas where they had once been submissive, women remained superior in the areas where their superiority had always been acknowledged. The gentleman might cease to be a gentleman but the lady remained a lady, with the result that (in USA more especially) the husband ended as the inferior. What has been lost is the wife's deference to the husband, that wisdom which led to her publicly accepting a male decision which could well have resulted from her previous and private advice. Wives have forgotten how to offer an open submission in return for a frequently decisive influence.

The sequel to this change in attitude is that the wife has lost control over the children. The Victorian wife used her husband's authority to quell the children; an authority which she had strengthened by her own example of calculated deference. The modern wife tries to reason with the children who therefore lack, from the outset, the security they need. She ends by hoping that the school will provide the discipline that the home has come to lack. This proves impossible because the sense of authority needs to be established before the age of five and quite possibly before the age of three. Schools can do all too little in this respect and universities can, of course, do nothing. The result is that we are faced in public and business administration by the need to establish some sort of authority over young people who may never have known any discipline at all. This is no easy task and we must feel sometimes that our failure is inevitable.

This feeling of hopelessness underlies the current talk about group decision. Do we *need* discipline after all? Perhaps the better way is to take a majority vote? Are we so sure, after all, that older people are wiser than the young? The fashion of today is to call youth into counsel and ask the advice of those whose careers have scarcely begun. Heaven forbid that we should be thought surly and despotic! We must also remind each other that the technological trend goes against the claims of seniority. Significant changes of method used to occur about once in thirty years. Each generation could learn from the last, make its own contribution and look forward to another ten years of superior knowledge and valued experience. Changes have now become more frequent, taking place within the decade, and the value of experience comes, therefore, to be called in question. Seniority may signify no more than being out of date and out of touch. It is the younger men who have been on the computer course and the present directors may not even know the language. It is doubtful, moreover, whether the present-day technologists will respond to any sort of leadership. They are absorbed in their own electronic world and unable to communicate with those who have not attended the same sort of polytechnic. There was a time for leadership, many believe, but that time has gone. There is no place for kingship, they claim, in the world of today.

This argument may be plausible but it is based upon boom conditions and a seller's market. What when things go wrong? Shall we talk *then* about group decisions? One thing to remember is that authority brings, first and foremost, a sense of security. The sailor on board ship sleeps during his watch below in the knowledge that the officer on the bridge is both wakeful and competent. He would be more restless if he thought that the appearance of another vessel, on a collision course, would be the occasion for calling a committee meeting and asking each member for his considered opinion. The soldier on active service can sleep as soundly on the assumption that the sentries have been posted and that an officer will be going the rounds. Nor is an industrial plant entirely different. It depends for its security on a whole series of safety precautions and the employee relies on the management to see that these are properly carried out. Without a measure of authority a railway line or coalpit can be heading for real disaster. Other establishments are less subject to risk, their potential hazards being more financial than physical, but this is not to say that risk is absent or that it may not sharply increase. But how can we supply then, in an instant, what we have for long dismissed as valueless?

Some people believe that leadership is a quality which you have at birth or not at all. This theory is false, for the art of leadership can be acquired and can indeed be taught. This discovery is made in time of war and the results achieved can surprise even the instructors. Faced with the alternatives of going left or right, every soldier soon grasps that a prompt decision either way is better than an endless discussion. A firm choice of direction has an even chance of being right while to do nothing will be almost certainly wrong. Starting with this premise the potential leader soon learns to make up his mind. It then remains to ensure that his action is based on commonsense. Having reached that point, the future officer must make his authority persuasive and acceptable. There is a technique to be applied and it is one we can describe with confidence. The secrets of leadership have to be rediscovered by each generation but they are simple enough in themselves. There are six basic elements and all of them may be acquired or improved by study and practice.

The first element is imagination. If anything is to be created, constructed, moved or reorganized, the man responsible must have a clear picture in his mind of what the final result is to be. Such a picture, formed in the mind's eye, is a compound of things we have actually seen elsewhere and on other occasions but now re-arranged in a different context. Taking command of a new ship, as yet unmanned, an officer will imagine the end result he desires to see in terms of efficiency. Remembering all that was best in his past experience he combines all together in a mental image. The reality may be utterly different but he has begun at least with an idea of what he is trying to do. Imagination is essential, and it comes first, for without imagination we are aimless.

The second element is knowledge. This is obviously needed to plan the route by which the goal is to be reached. But it is knowledge again which gives the leader the necessary confidence; the feeling that he knows what he is talking about. The world is full of people in positions of responsibility who are ignorant of their own business, possibly as a result of a too swift promotion, possibly from mere lack of brain. It is difficult for them to command the respect of the technically competent. They tend to feel vulnerable and insecure. To compensate themselves for their weakness they tend to indulge in fault-finding, bad temper, shouting and abuse. All this may be attributed by others to a poor digestion or a nagging wife. The fact is, however, that the bully has his own unconscious motive. He knows that there will be frequent mistakes in his office – as there have always been in every office in which he has appeared – and he wants to prove in advance that the fault lies in others and not in him. All those junior to him are disloyal, careless, idle and dense. His equals are incompetent, jealous, interfering and blind. Those senior to him are incapable, alas, of recognizing merit when they see it. Can anyone wonder that documents should be lost, that letters should be unposted, that dates should be forgotten and notices ignored? Heaven knows that he has done his best but he cannot be everywhere and there is no one else he can trust. Incompetence of this kind is often (not always) due to the man's basic ignorance. He literally does not know what he is trying to do.

So knowledge is important. The same can be said of the third element, ability. It is a word we need to define, making a sharp distinction between ability and skill. The skilful person is one who can do with relative ease what others will find difficult. He can play the cello, or score a century at cricket.When we go beyond skill, organizing the work of others – as in conducting the orchestra, or captaining a team – we need to display ability. Our own skill (which should be outstanding) is now less important than our capability to direct others. The man of ability is one who has the whole situation under control. Under him each man has been assigned to the task for which he is best suited and each knows exactly what his task is to be. There is a tidiness about the factory and office and a strong sense of economy in time, money and effort. But what, above all, distinguishes the man of ability is the hall-mark of artistry or style. Good organization is, finally, an aesthetic exercise; the fitting together of material and effort in such a way that no one is overworked and no one is idle. At the very centre of the organization's daily activity is an area of calm, where the ablest man of all is totally free from irritation or panic.

Very occasionally there appears in the world a person of exceptional skill or ability with the added quality of vision. This is genius and there is very little of it in the world. The more we can breed and train people of ability, however, the more certain it is that some will be exceptional; and the greater the number of these men, the outstandingly able, the greater is the likelihood that one of them may possess vision as well. For all ordinary purposes, ability is enough but the world offers occasional scope for genius. It is too often lacking, however, at the time and place where it is needed. What we need, perhaps, is a system for deploying what little genius there is available; such a system as only a genius could devise.

The next quality needed (for leadership) is determination. This means more than being grimly resolved to succeed. It is a quality which can be broken down into three elements. First of these and basic to the rest is the knowledge that the task to be accomplished is humanly possible. The general who has equipped and trained a sufficient number of troops and brought them, properly supplied, to the right place at the right time, knows that victory is within his grasp. To that knowledge he adds, if he is sufficiently determined, the belief that what can be done will be done. He has finally to reveal a capacity for conveying his confidence to everyone else. He must so describe the object to be gained that it seems worthwhile. In the light of his description the sacrifices must seem nothing, the probable losses trivial. From his attitude of calm certainty the rest of the team will draw their inspiration. For enemies in war or for rivals in business alike his supporters will feel something like pity. Could their opponents but know it, their opposition is futile, their doom already pronounced. Nothing can save them now from being outmanoeuvred, outflanked and outfought, disorganized, disrupted and dispersed.

The next factor is one that people today will not readily accept: ruthlessness, which many would like to replace by a diploma in industrial psychology. All experience goes to prove that the effective leader must be pitiless towards the disloyal, the careless and the idle. If he is not, the work falls too heavily on the willing men. The sense of belonging to a picked team is soon lost in an organization where the useless are still included. The element of fear is vital to authority and enters largely into the atmosphere of leadership. There are leaders who are loved as well as admired but that does not mean that they have never been ruthless. As their authority comes to be firmly established they may have less need to inspire fear but it was usually, perhaps always, an element in their previous career. To say that it is unnecessary would be totally wrong.

The last factor is that of attraction. This does not mean attractiveness in the ordinary sense, for that is a quality beyond our control. The leader has, nevertheless, to be a magnet; a central figure towards whom people are drawn. Magnetism in that sense depends, first of all, on being seen. There is (as we have seen) a type of authority which can be exerted from behind closed doors, but that is not leadership. Where there is movement and action, the true leader is in the forefront and may seem, indeed, to be everywhere at once. He has to become a legend; the subject for anecdotes, whether true or false; a *character*. One of the simplest devices is to be absent on the occasion when the leader might be expected to be there, enough in itself to start a rumour about the vital business which has detained him. To make up for this, he can appear when least expected, giving rise to another story about the interest he can display in things which other folk might regard as trivial. With this gift for inspiring curiosity the leader always combines a reluctance to talk about himself. His interest is plainly in other people: he questions them and encourages them to talk and then remembers all that is relevant. He never leaves a party until he has mentally filed a minimum dossier on everyone present, ensuring that he knows what to say when he meets them again. He is not artificially extrovert but he would usually rather listen than talk. Others realize gradually that his importance needs no proof.

But if it is true that leadership is an art which can be learnt, it is probable that it needs to be learnt fairly soon in life. The eternal difficulty in human affairs is to combine experience with youth, giving the future leader a chance to develop his gift. Our danger today is that we tend to lengthen our years of instruction, demanding ever more technical qualifications, until the man who qualifies is approaching middle age. And after twenty years of routine subordination the chance has gone for ever.

Chapter 9

BARBARITY

Is the beard returning? It almost looks as if it has. In various lands there are young men who have put the razor aside. Looking around us, we cannot deny that the hirsute tendency exists. Should the trend continue, what is still the exception might well become the rule. What would such a fashion indicate? Is it a matter of indifference or a proof of virility?

At first sight the changes of fashion in men's facial hairstyle would seem to present a story of mere confusion, the ebb and flow as seemingly pointless as the rise and fall of the hemline. But a mere glance at the history of dress-making must convince us that fashions may be, and often are, significant. The bustle had a psychology as well as a vogue; and the same is true of the beard. Worn among most primitive people, it became a feature of many ancient monarchies. It was nearly everywhere the symbol of maturity, wisdom and age, the tribal elder being thus distinguished from the beardless youth. First to rebel against this tradition were the Greeks, who came to place a high value upon youth, vitality and form. What began as a fashion was eventually the rule, Alexander the Great ordering his Macedonians to shave as a point of military discipline. His pretext was that the beard might be seized by an opponent in battle. His real motive was undoubtedly to emphasize the special character of that civilization he had come to represent. Orientals might be bearded, Europeans could not. It was this tradition that passed to Republican Rome, lending character to its age of greatest expansion.

But what did it signify? Why could it be thought to matter? It mattered as the expression of an attitude towards authority.

Under the ancient monarchies the robed and bearded patriarch was the very personification of dignity, the robe perhaps concealing a physical impotence, the beard possibly hiding the weakness of the chin. In striking contrast, very often, is the bust of a Roman senator, the face's character fully revealed. In still greater contrast is the sort of statue in which Alexander appears completely nude. The authority vested by oriental tradition in remoteness and mystery was entrusted, in the Hellenistic world, to a character and virility quite openly displayed. We judge personality chiefly by the eyes, mouth and hands. The bearded and bushy-browed prophet with hands hidden in his sleeves may have (for all we can see) neither intelligence, humour nor strength. In a more democratic society, by contrast, the elector may fairly want to see as well as hear the candidate for office, to recognize the cleft chin of decision, the mean or obstinate lines round the mouth, the slack signs of dissipation or weakness.

With the Dark Ages came the bearded barbarians, followed by the equally bearded adherents of Islam. It was when the fortunes of Europe were at their lowest (6th–7th Centuries) that the Franks gave up the razor; leaving all that remained of civilization to a priesthood which, simultaneously and significantly, gave up the beard. When civilization began to revive, after the year 1000, the clean-shaven face was its outward symbol. By 1200 all chins were shaven and would so have remained but for the crusades. Copying their Muslim opponents, many of the Crusaders came home mounted, clothed and bearded after the fashion of the desert. There were many beards in 13th- and 14th-Century Europe but the clean-shaven fashion prevailed after Chaucer's time; so much so that a statute of 1447 compelled the English in Ireland to shave so as to remain distinct from the Irish.

Progress is seldom uniform and there were inevitable set-

backs, the worst being attributable to Henry VIII, who grew his beard in 1535. This copying of a French vogue was widely followed, though with some resistance among the lawyers and clergy. To this day the judge and barrister are almost invariably clean-shaven and how many have seen a cleric with a moustache? Among the gentry beards began to dwindle again under James I, assumed the clipped or Van Dyck form under Charles I and vanished altogether under Charles II, who had only the slightest trace of a moustache. For Britain and perhaps for Europe as a whole the centuries from 1650 to 1850 represent the period of highest achievement. And for all or most of that period the clean-shaven chin was all but universal in the West. While a 16th-century writer could remark that, "Twas merry in hall when beards wagged all,' there were no beards to smear the ink on the Declaration of Independence. The United States and the British Commonwealth were alike founded by and for the clean-shaven; the Empire being mostly the handiwork, incidentally, of a society in which smoking was barred. Moustaches began to appear in the British Army after 1798 and were fairly in evidence at Waterloo, which proved the rule. Sidewhiskers finally became the badge of servitude, being restricted to the butler, coachman, footman, jockey and groom.

Modern western civilization met with its first major setback in the period 1845–50. It is difficult to understand why this should have happened but the fact is beyond question. It is obvious, for example, in architecture. At one moment (1845) people are building sensible, if spiritless, dwellings of classic design. A moment later (1847) they are building romantic absurdities which coincide, perhaps significantly, with the Communist Manifesto. This is followed at once by Napoleon III and the Third Empire fashion for pointed beards. For a time the stage Frenchman was recognizable by this affected appendage but the Crimean War brought the French and British

together. The French generals – St Arnoud, Canrobert, Bos-
quet, Pelissier – were all bearded before the campaign began.
The British – Raglan, Cardigan, Evans, Brown, Burgoyne and
Campbell – had shaven chins. When the campaign ended in
1856 the heroes of Britain were bearded cigar-smokers who
retired to live in hideous dwellings called 'Inkerman' and
'Alma'. Others, less heroic, could at least copy the beard (and
the cardigan) and did so. There followed the Volunteer Movement which made every man in Britain a soldier and thus
entitled, and at one time compelled, to grow a moustache. So
beards and moustaches were everywhere, the forest being
thickest in about 1880–90. The male face began to reappear
from the shrubbery in 1900, was clearly visible by 1910 and has
been predominantly clean-shaven ever since, with the beard
(not the moustache) allowed in the British Navy and the
moustache (not the beard) in the British Army.

One thing apparent from this historic outline is that the
clean-shaven face is associated with the West throughout its
periods of dominance. The beard has characterized periods of
decline and uncertainty. The beard was evidently the cloak for
hesitation and doubt; of which there was little between 1650
and 1850. How can that be proved? Consider again that last
bearded half-century, 1858 to 1908. Architecture was at its
worst, recovering only from about 1890. Art was all but dead,
recovering only as the century approached its close. Costume
was more stuffily unsuitable than at any time before or since.
Furniture and interior decoration reached a climax of incon-
venience, ugliness and bulk. The theatre was lifeless and great
music an heirloom from the past. Religion bulked large in social
life but doubts were undermining its basic doctrines; and while
the Americans were at war with each other the preachers were
at war with themselves. By every standard, this period was very
unattractive indeed.

But why was the beard so essential to this confusion? Because it was the thicket behind which the older men could hide their uncertainties. Challenged on the truth of Genesis, the elderly divine could retreat behind a barrier which might represent the wisdom of the ages. Questioned about army organization, the Commander-in-Chief could withdraw behind his beard, with a screen of cigar smoke to cover the movement. Questioned about sex, the Victorian schoolmaster could be evasively hirsute. Questioned by his wife, the Victorian immoralist could use his beard in order to blush unseen. The beard could take the place of wisdom, experience, argument or sincerity. It could give the elderly a prestige based upon neither achievement nor brain. It could serve, and did serve, as defence for the pretentious, the pompous, the dishonest and the dull.

And now there are signs that the beard may return. If it does, we may be sure that its purpose will be the same as before. The young men who are bearded now may be still more thickly bearded when they have reached middle age. And if they are baffled now in attempting to decide what they believe or are trying to do, they will be still more baffled in later life. Against the bearded ones of the future the ranks of sincerity should be drawn up as for war. Down with all this mystery and pretence! Let us see each other as we are!

Chapter 10

REVOLTING STUDENTS

The revolution at Berkeley Campus, University of California, took place in 1964–5. Its belated sequel, the removal of the President, Dr Clark Kerr, took place after the election of a Republican Governor in 1966. The revolt at the London School of Economics followed in 1967, the students protesting against the appointment of the new Principal, and has continued ever since. Commenting upon these events, more or less new of

their kind to USA and Britain, writers have agreed that they typify a widespread movement. There is everywhere, they say, a divergence between the generations, a breakdown of communication between parents and children, a failure of authority. In so far as this is true, the first person to comment upon it would seem to have been Plato. Observing how democracy in a city can turn into anarchy, he remarks that, 'The teacher in such a city fears and flatters the scholars and the scholars despise their teachers . . . And in general the youth resemble the more advanced in years, and rival it with them both in words and deeds.' (*Republic*, 8th Book)

Here is a picture of the situation at the London School of Economics and its novelty is as startling as anything can be that was first described in the 4th Century B.C. The teachers have flattered the students, who therefore despise them. The causes are perfectly known and the remedy is perfectly obvious. What is more interesting is the further question of why authority should break down in one particular school. Where all are subject to strain, one collapses first, and we can fairly ask why this one should have been particularly weak. Granted that the trend may be universal, the open disorder on any particular campus would seem to reveal a failure in leadership. Nor should we ask why this mistake or that was made when the riot began. Our concern should rather be with all that was *not* done over the previous decade. In the riding school we do not praise the good horsemanship of one who stays in the saddle when the horse bucks; for we know that under a good rider the horse does not buck at all.

When we consider these cases of anarchy, the most striking fact to present is the university's failure to apply scientific method to its own organization. A university is a society of people devoted to the furthering and dissemination of knowledge in all or most branches of learning. Its members believe, first and foremost, that facts should be established by inquiry rather than by assertion. Research is thus basic to academic thought and the same methods are applied to a range of problems in science and arts, as also, more recently, to problems of management. Whole departments are thus devoted to public and business administration, professors being as ready to advise the industrialist as the civil servant. As soon, however, as the university's own structure is criticized the professors face outwards like frightened sheep, banded together for mutual defence. Academic organization must remain as it is, the solid rock from which research workers can observe the ebb and flow of the human tide. Methods of objective investigation can apparently be applied to all subjects but the one. And yet the university deserves some scrutiny if only because of its role in offering advice. If its own administration is weak, who will listen to the counsel it may have to give?

Were we to apply management science to the university itself, as we plainly ought, we would have to realize at the outset that a university is more difficult to administer than any municipal department or industrial plant. It has, to begin with, a twofold purpose. Whereas a teachers' training college need do nothing but teach and a research laboratory do nothing but research, a university does both and must maintain a balance between the two. Its key personnel are not executives from the business school but wayward and eccentric professors, characters more remarkable for their brains than for their integrity, people whose first loyalty is not to the university but to their own conception of truth. These scholars are exceptionally difficult to handle, persuade or lead. Nor is the financial background to the university an annual balance-sheet, with its tale of profit or loss, but a complex pattern of public allocation and private benefaction, departmental grants and individual fees. Its students, finally, are young persons whose inactivity is exaggerated by the length of time they have spent in school and often given fresh emphasis by the mere size of the university to which they have gained admission. A reckless distribution of scholarships has relieved them of the obligation they used to feel towards their parents. Kept at school for an appallingly long period, they are often far older than their predecessors at college, as intellectually backward as they are sexually precocious. Problems of supervision and discipline are far more

difficult than they used to be or need be. This being so, and the
inherent difficulties becoming no easier with the institution's
development and growth, university administration presents a
formidable task to even the wisest and best amongst us. The
paramount need is for leadership, with all that is applicable
of political and managerial skill. Towards systematically
supplying what is needed, however, we have done practically
nothing. Applying no research to the nature of the task, we
have never applied even common-sense to the selection of
the men.

University chancellors and vice-chancellors and college
principals have the most diverse origins. Perhaps a majority of
them were once professors but others chosen have been civil
servants, headmasters and business men. A general preference
for men with academic experience is justifiable on the assumption that professors may understandably resent the authority
of someone who is totally unacquainted with the work in hand.
By the same logic, a station commander in the Air Force is
always someone who has flown aircraft in his time, the assumption being that nobody who has not could establish his
authority over those who have. Granted this basic premise, we
realize at once how simple, by comparison, is the Air Force
system of promotion. The really incompetent pilot breaks his
neck on the basic flying course. The psychologically unsuitable
are eliminated in advanced training, often at their own request.
Of those who qualify some are killed and some are plainly
better than others. In the course of years the natural leaders
emerge by a system of more or less natural selection. A similar
process determines promotion in the Navy and (perhaps less
certainly) in the Army. There is no comparable process of
elimination on the campus, where the casualties are negligible
and where ineffectiveness is not immediately apparent. Academic failure is spread over the years, offering no equivalent for

the torpedo boat aground on a sandbank or the jet bomber buried in the hillside. The academic incompetent is hard to remove and hard even to identify. The damage he does is spread over a lifetime, and seldom made obvious in any one moment of disaster. He can rarely be shown to have made a mistake; least of all when he has never done anything.

While academic failure is a mainly negative process, academic success is at least partly susceptible of measurement. There are Nobel prizes, acclaimed discoveries, brilliant books and crowded lecture rooms. It is admittedly difficult to decide whether one man is better in geology than another in music, but some means of comparison exist and some sort of choice can be made. If academic promotion, from professor to dean, from dean to vice-principal, were governed by known achievement, we might feel more confident in the result. But any such system breaks down at the outset with our discovery that Professor A does not *want* to be Dean or Vice-Chancellor. The most distinguished man on campus, he is not interested in administration but solely in (say) astronomy. That is not quite true of Professor B, the economist, but his ambition centres upon his chance, say, of becoming economic adviser to the government with a seat, very likely, in the House of Lords. As for Professor C, well known on television, he is seldom seen in the common room and has not attended a committee meeting for years. By the time we have found a possible candidate for dean, we may be far down the list so far as academic distinction goes.

Professor S, however (of Social Studies), undistinguished in every way, has long since decided that his future lies in administration rather than in research. His rivals for the office are Professors T, U, W and Z (heading the departments of Taxidermy, Unison, Welfare and Zionism) and for these too there is no tremendous future in their chosen fields of study. The one thing we know about the candidates for office is that they want promotion, probably (if not always) because they have failed in scholarship. We may reflect, finally, that their relative failure in their own subjects is no proof in itself that they are bound to succeed in anything else.

This may be a pessimistic view of the current scene, inviting the objection that some universities have nevertheless been successfully administered. Granted that this is true, the fact remains that the choice of a university vice-chancellor is far more difficult than the choice of an air vice-marshal. This being so, the obvious precaution would be to provide academic selection committees with some means of assessment. All that they have now is the word of the referees: 'Professor Z is eminently fitted for the post he seeks' – which may mean no more than that his present vice-chancellor wants to be rid of him.

What is extraordinary, however, is that the Air Force, Navy and Army use more scientific means to make an easy selection than the universities – the very missionaries of science – will apply to a choice which is infinitely more difficult. For promotion to general all sufficiently senior officers may be assumed to be candidates. The obviously unsuitable were eliminated long ago by retirement, transfer and court-martial. The work to be done is relatively straightforward and there is no real doubt about the object in view. The process of selection could not be more simplified. Even so, however, the Army, Navy and Air Force have interposed that invaluable institution, the Staff College. At some point in his professional career, the aspiring officer will compete for a nomination to the Staff College, work for a period on the theory and practice of command, study the problems of strategy and administration, and emerge with a grade from a final examination. Those not accepted and those who have failed will never rise above a certain rank. Those who have passed are eligible for a staff post, those who have achieved distinction are marked for higher command. All attending the course have been compelled to consider basic principles as well as current practice. The system is not fool-proof, for men good at passing examinations are sometimes good for nothing else, but any system is better than none. In so far as a peacetime test can measure an ability in war, the yardstick has been fairly applied.

Why should we not have a staff college for academic administrators? Why should no science be used in grading the scientists, no art in assessing the men of art? Such a college, like many another, would have a dual purpose. It could do research, on the one hand, in university organization, card-indexing the facts which its students might use. We know that Aristotle collected and compared the constitutions of 158 different states. Has anyone done the same with 158 universities? Is the constitution devised for a university population of 1,500 still applicable to a university of 30,000? We know that universities vary in student population from 1,000 to 100,000. But what size is the ideal, if we are to judge from results? We all know that the right size is exemplified by the university at which we took our first degree; but there ought, surely, to be a better criterion than that. We also know that the costs of administration vary between 5% and 10% of the total budget. What is the right percentage and why? The ratio between teacher and taught is wildly variable as between one college and another. What ratio is best? Should the sexes be segregated at undergraduate level? Should graduates be allowed to spend up to ten years in gaining their doctorate? A hundred such questions are answered differently at as many universities; not all, surely, with equal wisdom. In considering most of them we need, above all, to substitute fact for opinion. There is scope, therefore, for investigation, for comparison and study. That there is room for local variations, as between one school and another, is obvious. That there is, on the other hand, room for some standard solutions to universal problems is at least probable. Higher education is itself, therefore, a proper subject for reason.

The Academic Staff College would also accept, as students, such men and women as may choose to qualify for administrative office in a university or college. The syllabus might cover (among other things) chairmanship and committee procedure, academic finance and audit, the principles of architectural planning, the problems of student accommodation and the technique of public speaking. Whether the candidates for higher office would directly benefit is immaterial, for the main object of the course would be to evaluate the potential of each. The aspiring professor may have a creative urge, a real passion for staffwork and a genuine interest in human relations. He may, on the other hand, have an inferiority complex, a poor record in publication, a talent for flattering his superiors but a complete inability to explain anything to anybody. It is not beyond the wit of man to devise the sort of test which will reveal his character, his motives and his limitations. By the time each has submitted a scheme for faculty re-organization, dealt with a dozen case-histories, planned an extension to the library and made a commencement address, the instructing staff should have a fair idea of his capacity. Is he outstanding, good, average, mediocre or quite unsuitable? The fact should be obvious in three weeks but we might be extra careful and allow a month. No results would be published but each person completing the course would be given, confidentially, a final result. Only on applying for a higher academic post would he have to reveal his grade, and then only to the selection committee. It would still be possible for a university council to reject a man with First Class honours, preferring the last

Vice-Chancellor's son-in-law, graded Third Class (below average), but they would at least know what they were doing. They would also realize what they might afterwards have to explain.

Chapter 11

CRABBED YOUTH

Is this an age of opportunity for the young? The stories we hear would suggest that it is. There are companies which recruit young men for preference and give them managerial responsibility at the age of 28–34, sometimes with as little as five years of experience in the business. Is it generally true that youth is being given a chance? There are at least three reasons for thinking that it may be so. First of all, there was a low birth

rate for much of the period from 1925 to 1945, the result of trade depression and war. Productive people thus tend to be outnumbered by schoolchildren and pensioners and should retain a scarcity value until about 1980. In the second place there has been a disproportionate growth on the managerial as opposed to the manual side of industry. Supervisory staff, which formed perhaps 7% of the working population in 1900, amounts now to 11% or more. In the third place, the mere existence of recruiting firms would seem to indicate a shortage of talent. Instead of young men scheming to attract the attention of employers, it is the employers who are trying to attract the attention of the young men. Their advertisements are large, urgent and costly and they are obviously prepared for a high failure rate among the staff they can thus attract. One way to have met the shortage would have been to employ women instead but the actual practice has been different, for the women in managerial positions number only one per cent of the working population and this percentage has remained unaltered since 1900.

The trend in favour of youth is, in many ways, all to the good. The middle-aged among us can look back, very often, on years of frustration. We can remember, many of us, the old men who refused to retire, the years we spent upon trivial routine, the feeling perhaps that our promotion (when it came) was all too late in the day. We can recall the appointments made of men who were at once inexperienced and elderly, men who had spent their first years filing away documents, their middle period in taking the minutes at committee meetings, their early maturity in answering routine correspondence and now, when old, were given a responsibility for which they were totally unfitted. In politics we have occasion to deplore the same trend, with statesmen of many countries cluttering the political scene with the deadweight of their obsolescence.

One looks back, by contrast, to the heroes of an earlier period; to men who commanded warships or regiments at the age of nineteen or twenty, to one, even, who became Prime Minister at the age of twenty-four. These examples inspire but we should remember that men of this sort left school a great deal earlier and usually married (if at all) a great deal later. A general aged 32 might have had ten years' experience in active command. How preferable he is to a general aged 55 who has had no useful experience of any kind! For youth at the helm there is much to be said. As an ideal, however, it is difficult to achieve in a country where people tend to spend so long a period attending courses of instruction. To combine youth with experience implies an earlier start than many people achieve, and it often happens that a prolonged education can prove a decisive handicap. There are young men today who have made a million before they are 25. This sort of success depends, as a rule, on having left school at fifteen without distinction and without regret. Others attempting to do the same end, admittedly, in prison. The fact remains, however, that the self-made millionaire (unlike the well-paid executive) must usually start life in a slum.

Take the case of an imaginary young business man, A, who is appointed to a responsible position at the age of 28. Let us suppose that he married at the age of 23, graduated well from the business school at 24 and joined the company soon afterwards. Regarded as promising from the outset, he was moved rapidly round the organization and given a spell, latterly, as assistant to the Managing Director. Now, at 28 (the father of three children), he is made Sales Manager. Should he prove a success there is every likelihood of his being appointed manager of the company's new Zed Plant at Runcorn. His assistants in the sales department are B (aged 51), C (aged 43) and D (aged 37); all three rejected as candidates for the post he occupies. A's immediate problem is to gain the loyalty of B, C and D, ensuring that the sales graph will at once justify his appointment and ensure his further promotion. A has somehow to convince these older men that he knows best. Still more to the point, however, he must first convince himself. For the chief danger to A lies in his own sense of insecurity. Should he feel ignorant as compared with his immediate staff, he will reveal the fact in one of two ways. He will either seek popularity by making concessions and promises, or else he will assert himself by petty acts of tyranny. Other symptoms of instability may appear daily on the notice board – typewritten warnings which should have been delivered verbally (if at all) and directives which are classifiable as needless or futile. Where A does feel sufficiently secure it is because his aim is to better the company and not merely himself. If his chief concern is for the shareholders, clients and employees, he can point to further achievements in which B, C and D can share the credit. He cannot expect them to join in furthering his personal ambition, if that is his main concern, for they have no reason to prefer his interest to their own. The appeal must be to something that is beyond them all; some object in the light of which all animosities must be laid aside.

If carefully chosen in the first place the majority of those given responsible positions before the age of 35 should justify their promotion. But this policy, like any other, has its drawbacks as well as its advantages. Should it become known that the company's policy is to promote men aged 30–35, all men aged 37 or more will know that they have been passed over and are no longer being considered. This realization can be extremely bad for morale. Men who do not actually resign may still lose interest in their work. Others may feel embittered and may express themselves accordingly.

The trouble with men in this category is that the wife's disappointment may be fatal to the husband's further usefulness: B's wife will resent having to treat A's wife with a certain deference; A's wife not only being younger but prettier. Poor C's wife will be as restive but D's wife will be the most dissatisfied of the three. For D, remember, is *almost* young enough to be still in the running. What is the difference, after all, between 35 and 37, especially if your birthday comes late in the year? Even when young men are preferred, there is good reason to reserve some higher positions for older men. Granted that some must be disappointed to the end, they should still be allowed to know that they have a chance. A last retiring post of Director (Maintenance) might be kept as reward for long service. It would cost little to secure loyalty thus over the previous decade.

Another point to remember is that men promoted to responsible positions at the age of 30–35 may remain in the company for another 30–35 years. Provided that the industry is growing and developing fast, there will be new appointments for them as the years go by. But what if business should slacken? All the responsible positions will be filled, in that case, by men aged (say) 40–45. For the next generation of younger men there is no hope of a senior vacancy. Ten years later the same group of crabbed youth holds the field and no man of destiny has joined the company for the last decade. Ten years after that the company's senior executives arrive almost simultaneously at their retiring age. They retire over a five-year period and there is nobody to replace them. This is, of course, an exaggerated picture, for the board would have taken some action to prevent such a crisis. But the risk of youth at the helm is obvious. It could mean blocking all promotion for the youth of the next generation. It may create a dull period when everyone seems elderly, followed by a crisis (in 1995) when there seems to be nobody at all.

Time is the cure for youth and the brightest young men of 1970 will be the more experienced and cautious men of 1984. In a period of recession, incidentally, it may be experience and caution that you want. But there is another danger against which we need to be on our guard. For the men we promote at the age of 30 tend to be too much alike. They have started with a technical training designed to make up for their inexperience.

They have the language of the computer on their lips and their lives are programmed to the same pattern. They are not only graduates of the business school but are often from the *same* business school: pupils of the same professors in economics, cybernetics and automation. It is an initial advantage that they can understand each other. It is an ultimate drawback that they may all give the same advice. The boardroom table could be surrounded, eventually, by men whose outlook is too stereo-typed. Instead of studying the current problem from different angles (financial, technical, commercial, political, sociological and legal) they may all see it in exactly the same light. Their memories may all go back to the same lectures delivered in the same room and to the same examinations taken so successfully at the same time. Here again there is a risk of exaggeration but companies do exist in which people have been trained to think alike. The immediate convenience of this may bring with it an ultimate penalty.

We talk too much these days of the subjects which should be studied at school or college or on the course in business method. It is not the subjects which matter so much as the sense of ignorance, the eagerness to inquire, the method of study and the habit of thought. Education is something which should perpetuate itself and lead to further study of different problems. With side interests and the pursuit of casual information people with widely ranging tastes will diverge from each other. They will end with a valuable diversity of opinion, provided only that they begin with a capacity to develop. Men of the highest distinction usually turn out to be well-informed, not merely in the details of their own careers but in many other directions as well.

There are reasons, then, for doubting whether the early promotion of the young would benefit every endeavour at every time. Where the endeavour is new and where the field is just beginning to develop, there may be good reason to choose the young. But to make early promotion a general rule would be neither feasible nor wise. It would merely create a log-jam in the years to come.

Chapter 12

THE ABOMINABLE NO-MAN

Many of the basic concepts in public and business administration were first defined by Dr P. G. Wodehouse, but they are now so much a part of contemporary thought that their origin is often forgotten. No-one can now recall a time when Yes-men and Nodders were not sharply differentiated in the textbooks, but seldom is credit for this useful distinction given to the

thinker who first perceived wherein the difference lies. Among the few, however, who remember Wodehouse's first brilliant paper (read before the Royal Society in 1929) there is a feeling of regret that his attention was never drawn to the opposite sub-species; the No-men and the Shakers. One reason why his researches stopped where they did is that Yes-men operate *within* an organization while No-men are more prominent in its external relations. It may seem presumptuous to draw distinctions where so great a scientist as Wodehouse could perceive none, but there is no doubt that some classifying and defining would be at least convenient, even if we recognize, as we must, that it cannot be final. Recent research has shown that administrative organizations, whether governmental or industrial, have two vertical channels. There is, on the one hand, the channel through which the decisions taken on the highest level are filtered down to the pyramid's base. There is, on the other hand, the channel through which applications, suggestions and appeals make their way from the base to the summit. These two channels seldom correspond to those which exist on paper but research has shown that the chain of command on the executive side goes from the Chief to the Knowman and so to the Yes-men (Senior and Junior) and at last to the Nodders. The theory has been propounded that the incoming proposal is dealt with on the contemplative side by the Shakers, the No-men (Senior and Junior) the Don't-knowmen and, eventually, the Chief. There are two objections to this theory, however; in the first place, it does not tally with our experience. In the second place, it does not explain how any idea ever reaches the Chief at all. The truth is that the contemplative side of an organization is seldom entirely negative. What we actually find is that two types alternate at different levels. We thus find the Admirable Willingman alternating with the Abominable No-man. We find that Nodders intermingle with the Shakers.

To the man outside the hierarchy with an idea to sell, the effect is one of alternating despair and hope; an effect best to be described in narrative form. Picture, to begin with, the head office or Ministry. Beneath the visitor's left arm is the scheme, the plan, the blueprint or brainwave. Trembling slightly, he is shown into the office of Mr Jolly D. Goodfellow, who wears country tweeds and an Old Receptonian tie.

'Come in, Mr Hopefall. Take the armchair. Do you smoke? Forgive me a moment while I send for your file. Valerie, would you mind bringing the file on the Hopefall Project? I had it yesterday ... Ah, here it is! Thank you, Monica: you look very glamorous today – a lunch engagement? All right, we shan't expect you back until three-ish ... Now, here is the file, right up to date. I have studied your scheme very carefully and can see no objection to it. In fact, I think it most ingenious. We should all congratulate you on the method by which you propose to overcome the main technical difficulty. A neat solution, lucidly explained! The scheme has my fullest support.'

'We can go ahead, then?' asks Mr Hopefall, scarcely able to believe his ears.

'Yes, yes, certainly!'

'What — now?'

'Yes, immediately. Well, *almost* immediately. As soon as we have the Chief's signature. I foresee no difficulty of any kind.'

'You can't approve it yourself?'

'Well, no, not exactly. But I can advise the Deputy Assistant. *He* can approve it straight away; and I expect he will.'

'That is terribly kind of you.'

'Not in the least. We are here to serve the public, I always say; not to create difficulties just for the love of obstruction. We are definitely out to help all we can. That is our job ... Now, I have added my strong recommendation on the minute sheet. All I need do now is to sign it – so. And we might do well to accelerate the process a bit. Valerie, do be a dear and find me an URGENT label in red. Thank you, that's fine. See that this file goes *direct* to the Deputy Assistant. Come back tomorrow at this time, Mr Hopefall, and you should be able to go ahead on the following day. Ask for me personally and telephone extension 374 if you have the least difficulty. It has been a pleasure meeting you, Mr Hopefall. Goodbye for the present, and all good luck with your project. You have nothing further to worry about.'

*

On the next day, Hopefall is told that the Deputy Assistant can see him at 12.30. After waiting in the outer office, he is shown at 1.45 into the small bare room occupied by Mr Ivor Snagge, who wears deep mourning, rimless spectacles and a shifty expression.

'Ah, Mr Hopefall, I have been studying this scheme of yours . . .'

'I trust my memorandum sets it out adequately. If there is anything I can explain more clearly, I shall be glad to do so.'

'That won't be necessary. The proposal is clearly described. The trouble is – (Miss Tightlace – shut the window, please. There's a draught!) – What was I saying? Ah, yes. The trouble is that the scheme is impracticable, unacceptable and quite possibly illegal. It is, to my mind, *completely* out of the question.'

'Oh, but *why*?'

'Completely and utterly impossible. I should have thought that even Goodfellow would have realized that. On financial grounds alone.'

'But, surely –'

'Out of the question, Mr Horsfall. The objections to the plan are as numerous as they are insuperable. (Miss Tightlace – wedge some paper under that window – I can *still* feel a draught.) No, Mr Horsfall, it cannot be done.'

'Are you sure that you have the right file before you? My name is not Horsfall but Hopefall.'

'So you think I would deal with a matter of this kind without studying the right file?'

'Well, you hadn't the right name.'

'And that proves that our whole procedure is careless, haphazard and lax?'

'I never said that.'

'I think you did.'

'In that case you are prejudiced against me and should refer the matter to higher authority.'

'That is what I intend to do. In the meanwhile, I must ask you to leave this office before I send for the police. No violence, please! Your application is rejected. That is final, and you will gain nothing by abusive language. Good-day to you, Sir.'

Ten days later Mr Hopefall will be edging nervously into the presence of the Assistant Director, wondering what to expect this time. He need not have worried, however, for Mr O. H. Gladleigh is both helpful and charming.

'I have a minute here from Snagge but we won't take that too seriously. I expect you saw him about lunchtime. A most conscientious worker, you know, but a bit testy after midday. Now, about your proposed scheme, I can see no real objection to it. In principle it should be accepted. I only wish I could do that at once on my own authority. In view, however, of the points raised by Snagge, I think it will have to go to the Deputy Director. I shall strongly advise him to authorize the scheme, treating the matter as one of high priority.'

A week later Mr Hopefall will march confidently into the Deputy Director's office, to be confronted by a tall, thin man of haggard appearance staring hopelessly into some dreadful futurity. This is Mr Longstop. He holds the file limply and motions his visitor to a chair. There is a silence of a minute or two, and then Mr Longstop sighs 'No'. After another minute he mutters, 'Can't be done . . .' Then at last he asks:

'Have you considered all the difficulties? Financial? Political? Economic? Have you assessed the probable reaction overseas? Have you tried to judge what the effect will be on the

United Nations? I am sorry, Mr Hopefall, but I have no alternative. What you propose is, frankly, impossible.'

He will end by referring the matter again to higher authority. Nor need we follow the file to its logical conclusion. It is already apparent that the Admirable Willingmen alternate in sequence with the Abominable No-men. The final decision must depend, therefore, upon the number of levels in the organization or (to be more exact) upon the relative position of the level at which the decision will be made.

From a study of this administrative behaviour pattern it is possible to lay down certain principles to be observed by those who approach the organization. The first rule, clearly, is to persist. The applicant who left the building for ever after an interview with Mr Snagge or Longstop would never have met Mr Gladleigh nor spoken with Longstop's superior, Mr O. K. Oldmann. The best policy, it must be obvious, is to persevere until you find a Willingman.

The situation is one that we often encounter when shopping. The assistant says at once, 'No, we have no Sopvite Shaving Cream. There is very little demand for it.' The experienced customer perceives at once that the assistant is too lazy to see whether she has the stuff or not. He decides, therefore, to wait. He finds a stool and settles down with an air of limitless patience. In ten minutes the assistant, sick of the sight of him, produces the Sopvite, muttering that she has found an odd tube left over. She will in fact have had to arrange for the opening of a new crate but there is no need to comment upon this. The point is that persistence has won. In the imaginary examples quoted the various executives have automatically referred the proposal each time to higher authority. In real life they might not have done this. The technique, therefore, is to sit patiently until they do. It is needless to say anything much. Just

sit and stare at the executive until exasperation forces his hand. Inclination and habit will alike induce him to refer the matter to someone else. You will then have scored a point, for the other man can hardly be more obstructive and may well be less.

The second rule is to make use of the Willingman when you have found him. Your object this time is to obtain a decision and prevent reference to the next higher level. You will know from experience that a Willingman's superior is normally a No-man. You must, therefore, convince the Willingman that the decision can be his. The technique should be one of regret that so trifling a matter should have been allowed to reach so senior an executive.

'I am really ashamed,' you will repeat, 'that your time should be occupied in this way. It is satisfactory for me, I will admit, to discuss the question with a man actually responsible for making big decisions. One tires of argument with mere underlings. But this problem scarcely deserves your notice.'

Expanding in the warmth of your admiration, the Willingman may quite possibly sign his approval there and then, irrevocably committing his superiors to a policy of which they know nothing; and this is exactly what you want.

The third rule is to avoid wasting time on the No-man once he has been identified. It is a common error to suppose that the No-man could be convinced by argument and might eventually say 'Yes'. But that is to misunderstand the No-man's character. His automatic negative does not arise from any rational opposition to your scheme as such. He says 'No' because he has found that this is the easiest way and because he never says anything else. Should he say 'Yes' he might be asked to explain the basis for his enthusiasm. Should he approve, he might be involved in work resulting from the proposal's acceptance. Should the scheme prove a failure he might be held responsible for advocating it in the first place. But saying 'No' is relatively safe. It requires no explanation because those higher in the organization need never know that the proposal was ever received. It involves no work because no action follows. Nor can the scheme fail for it will not even be tried. The only danger is that the applicant may gain a hearing some other way; but even later acceptance of the plan need not worry the No-man unduly. He cannot be held responsible for any failure and will not be asked to aid in ensuring success. Few will remember his opposition and those who do can be told that the plan *in its original form* was impracticable and that its effective application, after revision, owed much to the process of healthy criticism to which it was subjected in the early stages of its development. The No-man has little to lose.

The successful application of the principles here revealed depends not upon argument as to the merits of the case but upon a preliminary survey of the organization. The correct procedure is to count the number of levels and discover where the No-men are placed. Make a chart of the whole structure indicating the No-men as so many black squares in what we can fairly describe as the crossword puzzle. Then plan your campaign so as to avoid the black squares, side-stepping from one Willingman to the next, and so reaching the lowest level at which a decision is possible. In an organization comprising executives who always say 'Yes', and executives who always say 'No', the problem is not one of argument but of pattern. The navigator does not argue with rocks; he avoids them. That this is the right policy is apparent to anyone who knows that the rocks (the No-men) exist. As against that, it would be wrong to imagine that these elementary principles comprise the whole of knowledge. The problem of nomanity, as here defined or at least described, awaits detailed investigation. Our researches have scarcely begun.

Chapter 13

THE LAW OF DELAY

There is nothing static in our changing world and recent research has tended to show that the Abominable No-man is being replaced by the Prohibitive Procrastinator. Instead of saying 'No' the PP says 'In due course' (scientifically, IDC), these words foreshadowing Negation by Delay (scientifically, ND). The theory of ND depends upon establishing a rough idea of what amount of delay will equal negation. If we suppose that a drowning man calls for help, evoking the reply 'In due course', a judicious pause of five minutes may constitute, for all practical purposes, a negative response. Why? Because the delay is greater than the non-swimmer's expectation of life. The same principle holds good in a case at law. A, divorced from B, demands the custody of their daughter (aged 17) but is told by counsel that she will be of age before the case can be determined. At the retail level, A is told by his ironmonger, B, that the lawnmower he wants can be delivered in six months (i.e., by December). All these are examples of ND in its simpler forms.

Where the urgent matter requires remedial legislation, delay takes on a new dimension. The judicious pause will correspond, nevertheless, to the life-expectation of the man from whom the proposal originates. If it is the divorce laws which obviously need revision, the Prohibitive Procrastinator starts by asking about the age and health of the Reformer whose Bill it is. Taking the age of 70 as the basis of his calculation, modified by actuarial factors, he concludes that Reformer A may expect to agitate for another eight years. Negation by Delay (ND) means the process of ensuring that 'in due course' (IDC) will

mean, in this instance, nine years from now. Realization that
the IDC is greater than the Reformer's expected life of agita-
tion (LA) is often enough to kill the whole idea at the outset.
For many altruistic men the knowledge that it cannot be done
in their lifetime is equivalent to the knowledge that it cannot
be done at all. Where a useful reform takes place, as must
occasionally happen, this is the result of the Reformer's living
and working for years beyond the limits of reasonable expectation. The Reformer may thus outlive the PP, whose
especial hatred is of reformers much younger than himself.
There are cases, therefore, where the IDC factor is less than the
LA and some half-hearted legislation is the result. But men like
Sir Alan Herbert have never been numerous and they are tend-
ing, in fact, to become extinct. The average reformer or in-
novator gives up more easily, leaving the PP in a position of
strength, ready to defeat the next proposal by using the same
technique. Delays are thus deliberately designed as a form of
denial and are extended to cover the life expectation of the person whose proposal is being pigeon-holed. DELAY IS THE
DEADLIEST FORM OF DENIAL. This is the Law of Delay. In
mathematical terms it is represented by the equation:
Where

> L = LA or the expected life of the person from whom the
>   proposed reform originates,
> m = IDC or the time elapsing between the first proposal
>   and the final solution,
> n = the number of extraneous issues brought into the
>   discussion, and
> p = the age of the Prohibitive Procrastinator,

$$x = \frac{(L+n)^m}{3p}$$

Then x is the amount of delay which is equal to denial.

At this point it is necessary to emphasize that the PP seldom says outright 'This cannot be done in your lifetime!' He allows this fact to emerge stealthily in the course of discussion.

'Our best method,' he will begin with apparent helpfulness, 'is to form a Committee on Procedure. This will produce an outline proposal, the various parts of which will be referred to sub-committees formed to deal with the legal, financial, cynical, technical, political, hysterical, statistical, ineffectual and habitual aspects of the scheme. The sub-committees will report back to the Committee on Procedure, which will then issue an Interim Report. This should be laid before a Commission of Inquiry which will assemble not later than 1975. It will be the object of the Commission to recommend the procedures which we should adopt in deciding, first of all, whether there is a case for proceeding further in the matter.'

Pausing for breath, the PP will complete, on the back of an envelope, his calculation as to how much delay will equal negation. Having outlined a process which will continue until, say, 1977, he realizes that 1980 is the target date. So he continues as follows:

'Supposing – and I emphasize that the question is more – much more – than a formality – *supposing* that there is a case for action, the Commission's final report will go to an inter-departmental Working Party, which will advise on the composition of the Planning Committee. It will be the task of the Planning Committee to approach the Permanent Under-Secretary of State, who will bring the matter before the Minister. Should his reaction be favourable, the matter will be brought up at the Party Conference at Skegness. It will be for the Party to decide whether the time is opportune, so soon before (or possibly so soon *after*) the General Election. In the light of that decision it will be for the Minister to issue a directive. He would not, however, at that stage, do more than accept the need, in principle, for further investigation.'

That is usually enough to end the matter without a single argument being used against the proposal under discussion. All the Reformer can see before him is an endless vista of committees trying to decide whether there is a case for making a preliminary inquiry into the terms of reference for a Commission. Comitology (the science of committee-sitting) is an old method of playing for time, but the techniques of delay have been strengthened in the modern world by the current emphasis on research. In matters scientific, the first rule, as we know, is to discover the facts. The same rule, as applied to human problems, means that a crime wave is not a matter of principle but of measurement. If Negroes riot in Los Angeles our first reaction is to count the Negroes, our second to decide whether they are as black as they are painted. That fact-finding is thus a substitute for decision is very generally known. What we fail to recognize is that fact-finding is also a substitute for thought. The months we spend in hearing the views of statisticians, psychologists, graphologists, sociologists, alchemists and alienists are not merely months of inaction. Their effect is to smother our thought (as well as our action) in waves of irrelevance. We shall have to realize some day that reforms depend upon the existence of reformers with a general as well as a specialized knowledge, upon people who are often a law unto themselves, upon people who say 'Why not?' more often than 'Why?' and refuse to listen to the PP's covert opposition.

Army officers used to be taught, and indeed may still be taught, how to make an Appreciation. In doing this, one used to begin (it might be) with a theoretical position of crisis. The enemy would be advancing from A towards B, the bridge being blown up at X and the railhead destroyed at Y, with all communication interrupted between you and the next higher formation. With shells bursting on all sides, the harassed officer

was supposed to sit down and write 'Appreciation' at the top of a sheet of foolscap, underlining it before going on to add the details of his Aim, the Factors which might affect its Attainment, the Courses open to either side, and the Conclusion to which he was inescapably driven. No marks were ever awarded for concluding that the Army was the wrong profession to have chosen in the first place.

There can be no doubt, however, of the value of this mental exercise. Whether or not people actually do all this in battle, the logic of the Appreciation has much to commend it. And one would suppose that the commonest mistake of inexperience would be in a misinterpretation of the facts. In fact, however, the real stumbling block is always the *Aim* paragraph. For most people it is far more difficult to decide what they are trying to do than to describe how they propose to set about it. As for the factors which affect the situation, as seen from either side, they are only relevant in so far as they relate to the aim. If the aim is wrong, nothing else in the appreciation will be right. This observation is as true in peace as in war and the born Reformer is one who considers his aim first and the statistical position afterwards.

With his aim clearly in mind what is his next step? Surely, a memorandum. But here lies one of the most dangerous traps in his path. In former times, and even, it is rumoured, today, he would seek to give his ideas the widest circulation and have them printed or duplicated in large numbers. Because it was uneconomic in time and expense to set up the type or cut the stencil more than once, he always ordered spare copies. Where 78 people were to have copies he would order 100, just in case more would be needed; where 780, he would order 1,000. But the spare copies represented a waste, deplorable for any administrator. The natural reaction was to distribute them to those marginally interested in the issue. But each time even more copies were added, for distribution lists like many things have an innate principle of growth. And, just as inevitably, the lengthening list extended to people who were decreasingly literate. More and more people at lower and lower levels were spending longer and longer time reading what concerned them less and less.

It is here that the Reformer who wishes to outwit the PP finds to hand an unexpected ally in the form of a piece of modern technology. By dialling from a suitable machine a precise number of copies of a clearly thought-out and convincing memorandum – the number calculated on the basis of the effective decision-makers in his way – the Reformer bypasses both delay and unintelligence at one stroke. He gets his views in front of the right people at the right time.

Memoranda come from those who have done their thinking beforehand. In three respects the writer of a crisp memorandum with a specific circulation has an advantage over the PP. He has defined his purpose. He has undermined the confidence, in committee, of those who have failed to read it. And he has provided, quite probably, the basis of what will be agreed.

Parkinson's Law of Delay cannot of course be avoided; it is as inevitable as the Law of Gravity. But just as it was within the bounds of human ingenuity to accomplish human flight, so, perhaps, there will always be a right way of getting new ideas off the ground.

Chapter 14

A CHRISTMAS CAROL

The Right Honourable Godfrey King-Wenceslaus, P.C., M.P., looked out from a window of his club and gazed thoughtfully across the park. Snow was still falling, blown by an icy wind, and the moonlight revealed only a single figure in that bleak landscape. It was that of a shabbily dressed man who was picking up sticks from under the trees and putting them into a sack, no doubt for fuel. 'Goody', as his friends called him, wondered that anyone in the Welfare State should be reduced to such poverty. He thought it highly irregular and doubted whether this firewood collecting was even legal. The only other member present in the Smoking Room was his own Parliamentary Private Secretary, an Old Harrovian called Page, and the Minister now called him over to the window.

'You see that hungry-looking fellow over there? I should like to know who he is and where he lives.'

The PPS had a word with the hall porter and came back with the information his chief wanted. 'He is known as wood-gathering Willie and is often to be seen round here. He lives over three miles away in a hovel long since scheduled for demolition. It is just this side of the new Ministry of Health and Efficiency – that high building next the Water Board's Office in St Agnes Road.'

'Thank you, Page,' said the Minister, still gazing across the moonlit park. 'I wonder,' he continued, thinking aloud, 'if it would be good publicity to ensure that this poor chap has a better Christmas than now seems probable?' Sitting down at the centre table, he scribbled a list of essential items beginning with a bag of smokeless fuel and ending with a bottle of nonvintage port. 'The gimmick would be that you and I would be surprised by the camera as we followed him home across the snow. What do you think, Page? A good idea?'

'My shoes are unsuitable, sir.'

'You will be all right if you follow in my footsteps – and I have goloshes.'

'Quite, Minister, but I venture to suggest that the idea is wrong in principle. If the welfare services have failed in this instance it should be our duty to start a process through the usual channels.'

'Ask the Member, you mean, to contact the National Assistance Board?'

'Exactly. Then the case would be properly investigated.'

'That wouldn't happen during the holiday season.'

'Not before mid-January, I should say, at earliest.'

'So it won't help this chap over Christmas . . .'

'No, sir. Not *this* Christmas.'

'I suppose you must be right. A pity, though, from the public relations angle.'

'The publicity might, however, have backfired.'

'The situation seeming too contrived?'

'It is a danger we should bear in mind.'

'Oh, well then, we'll scrub the whole idea. Draw the curtains, Page, will you? I don't want to see out again just now. I must rather study the welfare problem as a whole, undistracted by any particular case, however distressing. If there are loopholes in our system of social security there must be an administrative remedy. As basis for such a remedy we need the facts; the statistics, for example, of malnutrition during the winter months. Such a survey will take years to prepare; but the work needs doing. I'll write a minute to the PUS.'

Of course he was right. That is the approach favoured by the elected rulers of the modern world. All must be treated alike and it would be wrong to single out for urgent relief the one victim whose plight happens to be visible. He must clearly take his alphabetical turn with the rest. Unfortunately, as it happens, the poor man's name was Yule.

MORE ABOUT PENGUINS
AND PELICANS

Penguinews, which appears every month, contains details of all the new books issued by Penguins as they are published. From time to time it is supplemented by the *Penguin Stock List*, which includes around 5,000 titles.

A specimen copy of *Penguinews* will be sent to you free on request. Please write to Dept EP, Penguin Books Ltd, Harmondsworth, Middlesex, for your copy.

In the U.S.A.: For a complete list of books available from Penguins in the United States write to Dept CS, Penguin Books, 625 Madison Avenue, New York, New York 10022.

In Canada: For a complete list of books available from Penguins in Canada write to Penguin Books Canada Ltd, 2801 John Street, Markham, Ontario L3R 1B4.

LIFEMANSHIP

Stephen Potter

'All go-getters, careerists, snobs, cads and cut-throats will find this book invaluable, and so do I' – John Betjeman.

In *Lifemanship*, Stephen Potter formulates a way of life that allows even the most inept frauds to triumph in the most ticklish situations. There are ploys to be used in conversation, at parties, whilst wooing, sunbathing or playing tennis ... In short, this remarkable book has the potential to change your life *absolutely*.

All you have to do is take it to the counter and ask the pretty salesperson to wrap it up for you. As soon as you get the chance, take the book out of its bag and read it. Don't put it down – someone might pinch it. Alternatively, secrete yourself behind the section labelled 'Social Anthropology Amongst the West Kensington Cave-Dwellers' – no one will disturb you – and read at your leisure until your life takes on a new, sparkling dimension.

Also published:

ONE-UPMANSHIP

GAMESMANSHIP

Stephen Potter

'Anyone for tennis?'

'Sure, I'll give you a set or two – but I think I ought to warn you that my serves are going in like a charging bull at the moment. Still, I'll try to slow them down for you . . .'

Game, set and match to the Gamesman!

The point is, why play the game, when you can play *and win*? Read, mark, learn and inwardly digest *Gamesmanship*. Throw it at your opponent if all else fails – but Maestro Potter (for it is he who leads the way) will show you the whole Art of Winning Games Without Actually Cheating.

So go ahead and teach yourself the most effective ploys for court, course and board. Then go in there and make it pay off . . . May the best man win! He will.

Also by Cyril Northcote Parkinson

THE LIFE AND TIMES OF HORATIO HORNBLOWER

At last, the full story of Horatio Hornblower's epic career can be pieced together.

Unbeknown to the late C. S. Forester, the Admiral left a revealing letter and three boxes of documents to be opened a hundred years after his death.

Acting on inside information, C. Northcote Parkinson tracked down the documents a century later. To his delight they provided many of the missing links in the great hero's life.

Here is a companion to the Hornblower chronicle which will earn for its author the approbation of the legendary Admiral's many admirers.

Also by Cyril Northcote Parkinson

PARKINSON'S LAW

or The Pursuit of Progress

'Work expands so as to fill the time available for its completion'

This is it – the book with which a professor of history poured the healing poison into more than 700,000 ears and undermined the administration of big business and the civil service.

'A devilish book. No businessman should let it fall into the hands of his staff' – *Financial Times*

'He has thrown a thunderflash into the management parade' – *Observer*

'An extraordinarily funny and witty book' – Stephen Potter in the *Sunday Times*